LUXURY
HOME SELLING
MASTERY

Happy Publishing

Luxury Home Selling Mastery

Compiled and Edited by Erica Glessing

FIRST EDITION

978-0-9895554-8-7

Cover Design by Michael Samuel
of www.MikeSamuelGraphics.com

Published by Happy Publishing, distributed by Ingram
HappyPublishing@gmail.com

Happy Publishing

About the Home
Featured on the Cover of
Luxury Home Selling Mastery

Serenity Ridge is one of the largest private residences in America.

This world class estate offers a lifestyle like no other. Created with a discerning eye as a family and corporate retreat, this sanctuary is ultra-private and secluded yet close to corporate and commercial jet facilities, and all vibrant Denver and Colorado have to offer.

Resting peacefully amidst on 70 valuable acres with every amenity imaginable, no expense has been spared in this magnificent estate. It is a sanctuary of peace, renewal, refreshment and an entertainment masterpiece.

The timeless design encompasses 67,000 square feet including five kitchens, five kitchenettes, 11 en suite bedrooms, 24 baths, six wet bars and stunning guest apartments connected by a private tunnel. It includes the main residence complete with plush conference facilities, two levels of entertainment, including a bowling alley, climate controlled wine cellar, tasting room, two-tiered atrium pool and spa. Enjoy the decadent movie theater, dance hall, proscenium stage, game rooms, ice cream parlor and craft room. There are even several secret rooms.

The owner's wing is complete with secondary master bedroom, romantic balconies, captivating views, kitchenette and a spectacular library with its own: Board room, great room, fire place, office, bar, private bath and two walk-out balconies.

Enjoy an additional 9,300 square feet of exquisite outdoor living spaces, stocked ponds, waterfalls, spacious grounds, a staff residence, garage capacity for 30-plus cars, champagne scenery and breathtaking views of the Colorado Mountains. Renew, refresh, entertain and create the memories of a lifetime, Colorado style.

Cover photo courtesy of Carl & Christine Battista; photo taken by Kristopher Lewis.

Table of Contents

Introduction

Dear Reader,

Many real estate agents sit on the sidelines of the luxury real estate business, assuming that they're neither rich nor well-connected enough to get into that game. They might be mistaken. Money and connections help, but not all successful luxury real estate agents started out with them. In this book, some of the most successful luxury real estate agents in America will share how they built their careers.

I began my real estate career in 1974, in the midst of one of the worst real estate and economic crises in modern times. Interest rates were in the double digits. You had to wait in line to get gasoline. Economic activity, including the buying and selling of houses, was near zero. The country had not yet begun to recover from what President Gerald Ford called "our long national nightmare."

That's what the playing field looked like when I decided to get off the bench and join the action — what little action there was. My first office was in the corner of my father's plumbing supply warehouse.

We shared a phone, and I made my own signs.. Hard work, diligence, and a passion to succeed allowed me to excel in luxury real estate sales — and with those three assets, you can succeed too.

The contributors to this book took these three assets and added understanding: Each of them understands the luxury real estate client's needs and desires and has learned how to meet them.

Luxury home buyers and sellers approach the process of buying and selling luxury real estate differently from other people. That's not just because the price ranges they deal in usually have one or two extra zeroes; it's also because of their mindset. Here are some of the characteristics I've discovered that have helped me succeed in luxury real estate that have also helped the contributors to this book.

1. Luxury home buyers dream big.

They also understand that a dream in and of itself will not get you to where you want to be. A dream needs to be turned into a goal, and the quickest way to do that is to assign a deadline to your dream.

2. They create and execute plans of action and adjust them as necessary to achieve their goals.

The contributors to this book will tell you that luxury home buyers or sellers are people of action. They know where they want to be. They know how they are going to get there. They know where they are going to invest. They know who is going to help them acquire or sell the property, and they plan accordingly.

3. Luxury home buyers and sellers crave data.

Luxury home buyers never believe they have enough information, and they'll gather it from every source imaginable. It might be hard for people in the price range of the median home sale price of the United States to imagine that a luxury home buyer or seller will talk to the clerk at the hardware store, the server in a local restaurant, or even a landscaper work-ing on a local estate to get their perspective of the market. They might not always use the information they gather, but they want to have it. This rolls into the next characteristic.

4. Luxury home buyers and sellers have a network; they build on that network.

Luxury home buyers never overlook an opportunity to meet new people; they never refuse an offer of infor-mation, even if it appears to be of no value at the time.

5. Luxury home buyers know how to separate emo-tion and logic.

They know what, where and how they want to purchase. An emotional component is usually in play, but they're careful to not let emotion overcome reason.

6. Luxury home buyers and sellers understand the difference between value and cost in the marketplace.

With all of the data they have gathered, they have a keen sense of value and cost. The old caricature of the wealthy individual lighting cigars with $50 bills could not be farther from reality. Having worked with luxury home buyers and sellers for more than four decades I can tell you that they are careful stewards of their financial resources. They understand value in the marketplace. Lastly,

7. Luxury home buyers and sellers don't get lost in minor details.

They understand the big picture. They're less interested in floor plans, ceiling heights or style of residence do than they are in location, privacy, and amenities that can't easily be duplicated. You could always raze a structure, add a room, or take down a wall. It's a lot harder to create a certain exposure or a side-slope location, or add a beach dock. These people understand the important factors, work towards obtaining their high-priority desires, and let the minor details take care of themselves.

So, do just as these wealthy buyers and sellers would

do: Find a comfortable chair, get to know the experts who have contributed to this book, and discover more characteristics of wealthy home buyers and sellers. You'll see what sets these expert authors apart from their peers—and you'll be on your way to joining the game.

Jack Cotton

Luxury Real Estate Marketing Expert, Author & Speaker

Cape Cod, Rhode Island

Author *Selling Luxury Homes* (Tied-mark Press, 2010)

Chapter 1

The Mastery of Selling Luxury Real Estate

By Carol Staab

New York – Manhattan

As I sit in my mahogany-paneled library in my Fifth Avenue home overlooking Central Park, one of the most coveted views of all Manhattan, its majestic reservoir and the residential grand apartment buildings on Central Park West, such as the Beresford and the Eldorado, with their majestic limestone facades illuminated by the afternoon sun, I reflect on my journey to become a top luxury residential broker that began over 20 years ago. My first two years were spent as a rental agent for the largest firm in Manhattan at the time, Feathered Nest. In that short two years, I rented so many apartments that I was able to obtain my broker's license and began to acquire a vast grasp of Manhattan's neighborhoods. I started to develop an encyclopedic knowledge of the residential buildings.

Getting to the top was a long learning process that was fueled by extraordinary hard work, great ambition, obsession about the business, and deep heart-felt satisfaction that I receive from achieving my clients' goals of getting them the highest price possible for their home or finding them the perfect apartment for their lifestyle.

New York City residential real estate is unique in so many ways. New York City is the most densely populated city in the United States. Manhattan, a borough of New York City where I specialize, is an island that is only 22.7 square miles and has a population of 1.7 million. Most Manhattan residents are vertical dwellers living in high-rise buildings. The housing stock is made up of rental buildings, co-ops, condominiums and town houses. In the co-op – condominium mix the ratio is 80 percent co-ops to 20 percent condominiums. Co-operative ownership on this scale is unique to New York and foreign or non- existent in other areas of this country. In a condominium, people own their apartment and a percentage of the common areas. The condo owner receives a deed, pays monthly common charges, and real estate taxes. In a co-operative, people do not own the four walls and floor of their apartment but receive shares of stock in the co-op corporation that represent the square footage of the physical apartment that they occupy. Co-operative owners receive in lieu of a deed, a proprietary lease and are referred to as tenants of the cooperative corporation. They pay monthly maintenance based on the number of their shares.

Frequently I am asked whether it is better to buy a co-op or a condominium. In essence, the answer depends on your preferred lifestyle. Living in a co-operative is like being a member of a private club. A prospective purchaser of a co-op must not only submit a board package detailing all their financials, but also will need to have a personal interview with the board of directors. A co-op purchaser can be rejected by the board without given any reason – just as they can be declined for membership in an exclusive country club. You are probably wondering why anyone would subject themselves to such scrutiny. One answer is that if a purchaser is looking to live on the Gold Coast of Park to Fifth Avenue or Central Park West in one of the most sought-after prewar buildings built primarily in the 1920s, that have grand-scaled rooms and high ceilings, then they need to seek out a co-operative, because few condos exist on the Gold Coast. Very few condos can compete with these grand old co-ops. These luxurious highly sought-after co-ops designed by famous architects such as Rosario Candella, Emery Roth and JR Carpenter, are known for high ceilings, large entrance foyers, grand scaled living rooms and luxurious layouts. However, the most important reason that I have observed for people to buy into trophy co-operatives are to enhance and elevate their status by living at an important, exclusive address, like those on Fifth Avenue, and to gain access to powerful neighbors where they can forge important social and business relationships. So you can see, one of the prime reasons for buying an exclusive co-op is very similar to the reason people want to join exclusive country club.

The perception of luxury condominium ownership has changed drastically over the past 10 years. The first condominium built in Manhattan was the St. Tropez at 64th Street and First Avenue in 1964. The big condo building boom in the 1980s produced many midtown condos that were marketed mainly to for-eigners as pied-a-terres. In those days, affluent New Yorkers turned up their noses at the shiny new con-dominium towers that featured a lot of one- and two-bedroom apartments with small rooms. That all changed around 10 years ago with advent of 15 Cen-tral Park West, an ultra-luxurious condominium that was designed by the famous architect Robert Stern, who has a passion for the majestic classic old prewar residential buildings. 15 Central Park West was built to incorporate the very best physical features of the prewar luxury co-ops and to provide the most luxu-rious modern lifestyle amenities sought after by the uber affluent. There were New Yorkers who lived in the powerful co-ops on the Gold Coast of Park, Fifth and Central Park West who bought apartments in the 15 Central Park West. Gone for the first time was the stigma for real New Yorkers to choose living in condos versus co-operatives.   Luxury condominiums such as 15 Central Park West were gaining much respect from the wealthy and powerful New Yorkers who didn't feel the need to vetted by a co-op board and loved the idea of living in a building where they could enjoy luxurious lifestyle amenities such as a private restaurant, a valet parking garage, a movie theatre, a heated pool, a huge fitness center, a business conference room and room service.

Manhattan is not one big overwhelming massive city, as perceived by many visitors, but is one of 30 neighborhoods that are diverse and distinct in their composition, architecture and the lifestyle amenities each offers. The perception of stereotypes of certain neighborhoods have rapidly changed since neighborhoods are organic and always evolving. For example, Tribeca 10 years ago was a neighborhood of industrial spaces and just a sprinkling of residences. Now it is a very chic trendy neighborhood offering large loft spaces that attract young families and celebrities alike looking for a quiet luxurious understated lifestyle that includes great restaurants and leisurely strolls along Hudson River. The best way to see the neighborhoods is explore them on foot. If you run into me on the street don't forget to say "Hi".

My daily routine as a luxury broker in Manhattan is probably a little different than other luxury brokers in other areas of the country. Most real estate brokers outside Manhattan own their car to drive their clients to preview properties. Here in New York, I use a privately chauffeured car to transport my clients around the city. Most of my days are filled with entertaining and networking as well as meeting with clients. Several days a week you can find me at the famous Four Seasons restaurant, a New York phenomenon where I meet with potential and past clients. Julienne Niccolini and his partner Alex von Bidder are the owners of the Four Seasons, one of the most talked about restaurants in New York. It is the home of the power lunch. I have been a regular there for many years. Julian and Alex always treat my guests like royalty. The Four Seasons has the feel of a private club and I love conducting business over lunches there. There are countless famous people who lunch and dine there such as the likes of Barbara Walters, Henry Kissinger, Bono and Anna Wintour.

Competition to get exclusive listings in Manhattan is extremely fierce. At last count there are around 27,000 real estate agents in New York City, according to the New York Department of State. There are presently at the time of this writing about 4,000-plus active listings representing a record low inventory level. Only the best brokers excel in this kind of market. The lyric from Frank Sinatra's song New York, New York "If

I can make it there I can make it anywhere" says it all! In order to stay on top and be a successful luxury broker I take a very different approach than most of my competitors. I invest an extraordinary amount of time building and maintaining strong close relationships with my clients where they view me as their trusted advisor just like they would view their private investment banker or attorney. I offer my clients an elite level of concierge service that includes connecting them with a well-honed and researched A-list of people to meet their needs from A to Z. Also I live a similar lifestyle as many of my clients so I can truly understand their real estate needs.

My secret weapons for winning listings from my rivals are my creative custom marketing plans, and my track record for getting clients the highest price possible. I also have a great reputation for marketing expired listings that other brokers failed to sell and achieving in many cases record prices for my clients. A key difference of how I promote my listings is that I spend about 25 percent of my gross income on marketing. When it comes to their exclusive listings, many brokers are less generous with marketing dollars. This is a big mistake! My credo is that you have to spend money to get the best results! An excellent example of how I market differently to achieve the highest price is shown in my creative and fabulously produced property videos. I have a video produced for all of my luxury listings where I personally narrate the tour and am able to engage buyers' interest in the property. Very few Manhattan brokers do this! The following is a fine case where a property video resulted in an all-cash $8.3 million signed contract from a Chinese buyer. A broker came to preview my exclusive listing in the 900 block of Park Avenue, a beautiful triplex with a private garden and terrace designed by a renowned landscaper. The triplex was in a luxurious doorman condominium. The broker said that she had a buyer from Beijing who was very interested in the triplex and wanted her to preview it. I asked the broker when her customer could come and see it. She told me that it may not be for another month! I told the broker that I had other interest in the triplex and that her customer would need to make it a priority to come and see it as soon as possible, or she would lose the opportunity to purchase it. I asked the broker if she sent her customer the video tour that I had online for the property and she said no. I urged her to email her the video and she complied. The next day I received a call from this broker and she was very excited. She said "You won't believe what just happened! My customer saw your video of the property, fell in love with the triplex, and has authorized me to give you her offer!" The negotiated offer was $8.3 million all cash closing in 60 days! The buyer flew to New York two days later to meet with her attorneys to review and sign the contract. My clients were so ecstatic that they sent beautiful orchids the same day the contract was signed. The video cost $900 to produce and the outcome was an $8.3 million deal!

Getting real estate sales to close in Manhattan can be complex, and presents challenges unknown in other parts of the country. It requires a seasoned broker who has many years of experience in the trenches, and has the ability to come up with creative solutions to see the deal through, from the accepted offer to the closing. It also requires extreme persistence and doing whatever it takes to get the deal done.

The following stories of some of my most challenging deals will illustrate problems that can occur when buying and selling residential real estate in Manhattan.

My sale of a large two-bedroom condo with Central Park views at Citispire many years ago seemed to be going well until the time of contact signing. I represented both the seller – a man from the Middle East who lived at Trump Tower – and the buyer, a CEO of an insurance firm and his wife from Los Angeles. There were two young men who were tenants living in the apartment. The buyers wanted to close in 30 to 60 days. At this time, the seller confided in me that his tenants were three months behind in paying the rent. He told me that he had taken legal action against his tenants, and that his attorney advised him that it could take him six months to evict them. The deal was going to die unless I did something to try to persuade the tenants to move out ASAP. What could I do? All of a sudden an idea came to me! I told the tenants that a contract of sale was signed. I let them know that I was also representing the new owners and that they wanted me to get access to have the apartment cleaned. I convinced the tenants they had to move right away because their lease was no longer valid and that the new owners were going to be moving in very soon. That said, by the time I came with the cleaning service they had moved out! But then another issue popped up. The wife insisted on having a washer and dryer in the apartment. I recalled seeing other apartments in the building where there were washers and dryers, so I thought it would be a no brainer to get them installed. I consulted with the super who told me that the washers and dryers that I saw in other apartments were "grandfathered" and new washers and dryers could not be installed. Again I faced another obstacle that was going to kill the deal. I told the buyer that washers and dryers couldn't be installed. She insisted that they wouldn't go ahead with the purchase unless there was a washer and dryer in the apartment. Then I thought of a solution that might work. I had a coffee with the super and I told him that I was very upset that my buyer was not going to go ahead with the deal unless a washer and dryer could be installed. I asked him if he could see some way of making it happen. I kept working with him on the possibility of the washer and dryer some-how being grandfathered in. I had them delivered to the building in plain boxes so that they couldn't be identified. The washer and dryer were installed as if by magic and the deal closed. I can't really share any more about how this all happened, but where there was a will, there was a way, and cash changed hands. The buyers and sellers were very happy and the sale resulted in many referrals.

Not long ago, an owner of a condo who lived in London and owned an apartment at 1049 Fifth Avenue asked me to meet with him to discuss selling his apartment. When we met he looked depressed and I asked him if anything was wrong. He told me that he had just come from his attorney's office and received bad news that was going to prevent him from listing his apartment with me for perhaps another six months. The news was that the very high profile public New York political figure that was his tenant was four months in arrears in his rent and it could take six months to legally evict him. I told him that I would give his problem some serious thought. This wasn't going to be easy since his tenant was very savvy. My first suggestion to the owner was to offer his tenant an incentive to move out such as forgiving the four months of unpaid rent. That didn't work. The tenant said his wealthy father was ill and pleaded with my prospective client to be patient. He told him that he was going to inherit a ton of money and all would be well. The tenant had a long history of having negative news written about him in the media. My second solution that I gave to my prospective client was that he inform his very famous tenant that unless he moved out ASAP that a story may just get into the real estate gossip column of The New York Post that he was four months behind in his luxury Fifth Avenue condo sublet. That said, the tenant moved out a week later! The fear of potential public embarrassment was a great motivator. I ended up selling the apartment for an excellent price and my client wrote me a great reference letter.

A 1049 Fifth Avenue Penthouse was on the market a year ago with a high profile broker who is referred to as the queen of Manhattan real estate. The penthouse was a grand 3,600 square feet, three bedrooms, four baths, plus two libraries, a staff room on the third floor and included two storage units. The penthouse had 360- degree breathtaking views of Central Park, the reservoir, and iconic buildings such as the Empire State and Chrysler buildings. The apartment was being sold by the trustees. One morning I was sitting at my computer looking at the penthouse listing that was about to expire feeling puzzled as to why this trophy penthouse didn't sell. Just then my phone rang. It was one of the trustees and her husband calling me to tell me that their experience with their broker had been a disaster. They told me that they were extremely frustrated and that the penthouse was rarely shown and when it was shown it was shown by someone else on this broker's team. After I took over the marketing of the penthouse, I was able to obtain four offers, including all-cash full asking sales price of $14,950,000, a record $4,185 a square foot for the building.

The last story that I want to share with you is about how a celebrity can add a certain cache to a listing and can create a big media buzz about a property even if by accident! This unit inside of 1049 Fifth Avenue is a 3.400 square-feet, four-bedroom, three and a half bath condominium with a grand-scaled living room that is so large that my client's baby grand piano takes up just a small portion of the room. All the public rooms including the living room, dining room, library and breakfast room all have stunning Central Park and reservoir views. On a cold December day last year close to Christmas Eve a very famous celebrity in the music business and his wife came to see the apartment. He sat down at my client's baby grand piano and began to play. Somehow the news of his seeing the apartment got out to The New York Post's famous real estate gossip column and from there the news went viral. There was an article in the Real Deal, Business Insider, and Curbed.Com etc. Confidentiality and secrecy plays a big role in Manhattan luxury real estate but sometimes news gets out in spite of your best efforts. Fortunately famous entertainers, such as Sir Paul McCartney, the legendary member of the Beatles, is used to being in the public eye.

So as the sun is starting to go down and the city lights illuminate the opportunities of New York City, from my view overlooking it all from my apartment on 5th Avenue, my phone rings and it is an accepted offer on the above apartment however the potential buyer wants to know if the baby grand piano can stay, hmmm!

This is only a tiny window into the world of luxury Manhattan residential real estate. For more stories on the fascinating art of making the deal please visit www.CarolStaab.com and click on Carol's Manhattan Luxury Real Estate Blog. Here you will also find my newsletter "The Pulse On Manhattan Real Estate".

ABOUT THE AUTHOR: *Carol Staab*

Carol Staab is a top Manhattan luxury residential real estate broker since 1992. She is the winner of the prestigious 2013 Douglas Elliman Platinum Award ranking her as one of the top brokers in Douglas Elliman, the largest and number one residential real estate firm in New York City. Carol is a member of the prestigious Who's Who In Luxury Real Estate whose members must be in the top 10 percent of their firm and top 10 percent of their local market. She is a NYRS

(New York Residential Specialist) who is board certified by the Real Estate Board of New York. It is the highest professional designation awarded only to the top tier of New York City brokers who have successfully completed an advanced graduate program through the Real Estate Board of New York. She is also a member of Haute Living Residential.

Carol has an excellent performance history for getting her clients the best possible results. She designs very aggressive creative marketing plans to promote her exclusive luxury listings globally through her prestigious real estate networks. An excellent example of the success of Carol's creative marketing is the property video of 985 Park Avenue that has been viewed over 1000 times! The video was key in attracting an all cash foreign buyer who made an $8.3 million offer after watching the video without seeing the property!

 One of the amazing things about Carol is how many clients have hired her over the years to market and sell their luxury Manhattan homes without ever meeting her in person. Carol's clients say that her outstanding track record and reputation gave them a high level of certainty that she would get them great results. To learn more about Carol visit www.CarolStaab.Com or contact her at cstaab@elliman.com or 212-891-7205.

Chapter 2

Getting to #1 in Luxury Real Estate, Park City Style

By Paul Benson
Park City, Utah

My career in real estate began in 2004. I was living and working in Newport Beach, California, and decided to spent a few months observing the market and educating myself about the ins and outs of the luxury real estate market.

At the time, I knew that if I was going to dive into the world of real estate, it would have to be in a market where I would have the greatest opportunity. I chose Park City, Utah, not because of its scenic mountains and great skiing, or its world-class golf resorts, but rather because I believed it had great potential and presented a unique opportunity for expansion. Park City is a tourist town, attracting a large population of high net worth resort enthusiasts every season. There are new faces searching for properties every day that have no affiliation with a specific real estate agent. If you match that with a large inventory of multi-million dollar properties, plus a high demand for ownership, you have an opportunity in the making.

I came from a competitive sales industry that was marketing-based. My first impression of Park City was that there were few real estate agents willing to invest in marketing in a big way. I felt this was a big injustice to the client. Taking a multi-million dollar home listing, putting it on the local multiple listing service (MLS), and skiing the slopes until it sold hardly seemed like a long-term formula for success. I decided that I was going to be a different type of Realtor®, setting the standards for the world-class marketing of luxury real-estate in a town that was ripe with opportunity and potential. With only a 30-minute drive to a major international airport, and plans in progress for new large 5-star hotels that would attract luxury buyers from across the globe, I saw an opportunity I could not miss, so I joined Prudential Utah Realty – and the rest, as they say, is history.

My strategy those first few years was to build a presence in the local market through charity sponsorships, through the local newspapers and magazines, as well as by hosting events that would demonstrate that my team would do a first class job selling luxury homes. I knew I had to back this up with knowledge, so I read real estate books every day. I studied the market meticulously, continuously observing and analyzing the trends. I became an expert in the inventory and transactions in my area and made it a point to know who purchased which home, at which time, and at what price, anywhere in town.

As the market heated up in 2005 and 2006 I began tracking buyer trends and analyzing luxury buyer profiles. Based on my research, I focused my marketing efforts outside of Utah to feeder markets, targeting luxury buyers looking for homes in the Park City area. At the time, I was one of the select Realtors® in the state of Utah that had a regional marketing strategy with an advertising and marketing budget that far exceeded any of my competitors.

This business model proved to be a success, and business continued to thrive at a steady pace. Although I was new to the market, I was ranked as one of the three top producing agents in the state my first three years selling real estate in Utah. This proved that my business model worked. I earned over $5 million in personal income my first three years as a Realtor®. More importantly, I was also making money for my clients, and I soon realized how loyal clients can be when you make a positive contribution to their bottom line.

I expanded my businesses model beyond marketing luxury real estate and began building a separate business with a focus on real estate investments, helping clients to identify the best investment opportunities in town. The investment side of my business grew quickly, as I became involved in large projects including the sale of a $200 million ski resort, as well as a large development on an island in the Bahamas. This experience brought me into contact with many of the world's wealthiest individuals. As my sphere of influence grew, so did my residential real estate business, and my listing numbers began to surge. I began listing and selling $10 million, then $20 million and up to $50 million properties. To this day, there are very few agents world-wide who experience this thriving business model and volume of luxury real estate properties that I currently handle.

Then the Lehman Brothers crash came, and one of the greatest recessions in the history of our country. In order to succeed, I realized that relations with banks and understanding the short sale market would be pivotal and would drive business for a few years. I restructured part of my business to focus on this area and survived. My large portfolio of luxury listings remained intact, and it meant that I would need an infusion of a significant marketing and advertising budget to promote these listings regardless of the recession. I had to make a decision: to invest in the future or live for today. I chose to focus on the future, creating a plan that allowed me to live off of short sale revenues and invest all revenues from selling luxury homes back into a comprehensive and highly targeted marketing plan designed to expand my business. The magazines had slimmed down, and I stood out. I became one of the few real estate industry to advertise. As a result, I was able to negotiate very attractive rates, and before I knew it, I was actually marketing my luxury listings more during the recession than prior to the market slow down. The advertising dollars paid off, and my portfolio of luxury properties began to grow again. As I began listing more luxury homes, it became apparent that in order to truly serve my sellers, I would need to effectively target luxury buyers outside the United States.

To expand my global reach, I joined Sotheby's International, a real estate brokerage firm with a local presence in over 40 countries and brand recognition in the global luxury market that is second to none. Switching to Sotheby's International translated into immediate global exposure for my portfolio of listings that had grown to over $500 million in 2011.

As a result of my targeted advertising during the recession, my portfolio of listings was unmatched, and had expanded to include luxury homes, condos, ranch properties and land development parcels. The Sotheby's International cutting-edge, online marketing strategy guaranteed my luxury listings global exposure. The opportunities seemed endless. My listings were now featured on over 90 websites. With a portfolio of 100 listings, this meant that I could be found over 900 times on any given moment on the internet before I even pushed for promotion. I added a social media specialist to the team to capitalize on this global exposure. My listings were now also being featured regularly on the covers of national luxury real estate magazines such as the DuPont Registry and The Rob Report, and I was being interviewed by international power houses such as the NY Times and The Wall Street Journal as an expert in the luxury real estate market.

I began traveling the globe to network and connect with other agents, taking advantage of the Sotheby's International brand and the global networking opportunities that this presented. I hosted events for top banks, CEOs and celebrities at the Sundance Film Festival, as well as sponsoring charity golf events in Lake Tahoe for the world's top athletes, just to name a few. Every new listing, every event, every new ad and magazine cover created new contracts and new opportunities. My business expanded to include the sale of hotels and commercial property. In 2012 and 2013, I was the top selling commercial agent for Park City, as well as the top selling residential agent. I have been involved in 18 of the last 25 development sales in Summit County. I have consistently ranked number one in the state over the past three years, and also ranked as one of the top 100 real estate agents in the US for the past three years in a ranking by the Wall Street Journal.

Today the business model I put in place 10 years ago continues to thrive. I am just as committed to my business and my clients today as I was 10 years ago. People often ask me how I do it and want to know the secret to the steady growth of my business. It goes without saying that I love what I do. That is no secret. I believe that high net worth buyers are not looking for a house particularly when buying a second home, but rather seek a certain lifestyle. I help my clients find a home that matches their lifestyle choices. It's all about knowing how to expose extraordinary homes with extraordinary lives all across the globe. Whether it is luxury home for skiing, ranching, or farming, or a golf course lifestyle a luxury home buyer desires, there is always an extraordinary home that fulfills that need. I don't see myself as selling homes but rather a lifestyle. The right home for the right buyer always sells itself. Beyond unlocking the door, a great house needs no help from me.

What I do is offer my extensive experience in negotiations that focus on both sides coming away with a win.

I now travel across the globe and within the United States networking and building a global brand and implementing the business model I used for Utah on a national level.

I strongly believe that there is a niche for someone that has the expertise to provide consulting and marketing services for luxury properties matching extraordinary properties with extraordinary lives anywhere in the world. There are very few people that invest the time to travel to various markets and study real estate the way that I do. My consulting opportunities now take me to places such as Lake Tahoe, Telluride, Los Angeles, Florida, The Bahamas, France and Dubai. I have found that no matter where you are in the world, you will encounter real estate agents trying to talk a buyer into a bad investment or a seller into selling their home under market value. My goal is to educate people on how to make money in real estate and where to get exceptional and accurate advice. Real estate is my passion. I am thrilled to have the ability to connect buyers and sellers from across the globe and I love sharing these experiences. This is the side of my business that I will never stop growing.

ABOUT THE AUTHOR: *Paul Benson*

Paul Benson has been consistently ranked as a top producer in real estate both locally and internationally since he arrived in Park City in 2005. Named #1 by the Park City Board of Realtors® in 2011, 2012, 2013, and 2014. Paul was recently recognized on "The Wall Street Journal" and REAL Trends Inc.'s The Thousand, a summary of the top one thousand independent real estate agents and teams in the United States. He is ranked 45th of 250 on the Top

Sales Professionals by Volume list and number one in Utah, with more than $136 million in sales volume. Paul has established a solid reputation and track record representing luxury real estate buyers, sellers and developers from across the globe.

A seasoned sales, business development and marketing executive with 20 years of experience in the luxury market, Paul has successfully negotiated the sales of multi-million dollar properties including the 2011 purchase of 5000 acres at the Canyons Ski Resort and the marketing of a 1,400 acre large density Bahamian island project.

With one of the largest international marketing budgets of any broker, Paul's luxury listings have graced the cover and pages of regional and international magazines and publications such as the Robb Report, Unique Homes, Dupont Registry, The Wall Street Journal and The New York Times to name a few. Paul also hosts a number of annual events for high net worth clients including Sundance Film Festival and American Century Golf Tournament in Lake Tahoe creating even more exposure for his business. Paul and his team currently have over 80 luxury home and land listings with over a half billion in dollar volume. The Benson team has successfully sold over $840,000,000 in volume, closing over 800 transactions in the past ten years.

Respected as an expert in the luxury real estate market, Paul is regularly quoted in industry magazines and publications focusing on high net worth buyers and sellers. With a global network, Paul is uniquely positioned to connect extraordinary people with extraordinary lifestyles. His 2013 networking events took him to cities across the globe including Hong Kong, China, Monte Carlo, London and Dubai as well as a variety of cosmopolitan cities across the U.S. His affiliation with Summit Sotheby's International Realty enables Paul to provide maximum exposure for his clients' properties to potential buyers from across the globe. Contact Paul at www.ParkCityHomeSearch.com.

Respected as an expert in the luxury real estate market, Paul is regularly quoted in industry magazines and publications focusing on high net worth buyers and sellers. With a global network spanning from the U.S. to Europe and China, Paul is uniquely positioned to connect extraordinary people with extraordinary lifestyles. His 2013 networking events took him to cities across the globe including Hong Kong, China, Monte Carlo, London and Dubai as well as a variety of cosmopolitan cities across the U.S. His affiliation with Summit Sotheby's International Realty and their world-wide network of offices and agents enables Paul to provide maximum exposure for his clients' properties to potential buyers from across the globe.

A native of Killington, Vermont Paul and his wife Alisha are proud parents of four children. Paul enjoys the Park City outdoor lifestyle including skiing, biking, golfing, fishing and motorcycle riding. Let Paul put his experience, knowledge and extensive global network to work for you.

Chapter 3

Everyone Wants to Make It

By Catherine Marcus

Beverly Hills, California

Everyone wants to "make it". Human beings are different in a lot of ways, but the American brain can be very predictable. No matter what kind of person you meet, no matter what field, when you shake someone's hand you are shaking the hand of someone who indulges in fantasies of riches, fame, notoriety, and social ascendance. These are the dreams of almost every human being; but why do so many people, in so many fields, instead flounder in dead end jobs with little growth? Because for many, these same brains that fantasize of endless success will also tempt us towards short cuts, laziness, and apathy. One can choose to write this off as cruel irony and succumb to these patterns or push against them at every opportunity — knowing that if you do you will separate yourself from 99 percent of the population. Entering the intensely competitive field of real estate in one of the most cutthroat zip codes in the world, I could have allowed my brain an incredible amount of excuses — "I don't know anyone in Silicon Valley!", "The competition here is just too fierce!" "I've never done this before, it will be fine if I don't give it my full effort" — and the bitter truth is that others would have enabled me. This is a trap so many fall in when it comes to Real Estate, but these are temptations that I refused to indulge. I pushed myself to succeed, used my God given savvy to get ahead, and constantly sought ways to better myself — and in 2012, my discipline paid off when I sold the most expensive single family home in the United States. Yes, everyone wants to make it, but so very few have the drive to create it.

My path towards real estate was an unconventional one, my collegiate degree in physics to residency in LA do not exactly match the pedigree of someone who would go on to sell houses to Silicon Valley bourgeois. I ascribe a good deal of my real estate skills to my background in technology — I left college with a degree in physics from Georgia Tech and a job at Satellite Network systems. Back then, technology was still a somewhat niche field; far from today's saturation of apps, smart phones, and laptops. Instead, technology to most people was still an abstract, vaguely geeky idea. It was this hurdle that helped me hone my skills in sales; I had to sell people their technology, which at that time was like selling a harpoon to a whale. Thus, I developed the invaluable skill of making a client feel comfortable with a product they had limited experience with. I had to make aggressively inaccessible products seem consumer friendly, and my sales expertise grew all the stronger. But I knew tech wasn't my first love, so I took all the knowledge I had garnered and translated it to a field that I would make my millions in: Real Estate.

Origins in Silicon Valley

 I relocated to Silicon Valley after a brief stint in film, and found myself at a bit of a career crossroads. The atmosphere of Silicon Valley reflected my anxiety — much like all those tech geniuses getting paid in paper clips, I knew that I was on the cusp of something great but wasn't quite there yet. I had little guarantees other than my raw talent, immense drive, and a determination to achieve greatness, but it would soon be obvious the path I was destined to take. Before I even took a training class, I would go to open houses every Sunday. I had no reason to go — I loved my home and had no intention of moving — but something about the untapped potential of a house on the market made me infinitely enthusiastic. Eventually, the day came when I put my own house on the market, and felt an immense dissatisfaction with the personalities in charge of selling my home. This distaste proved to be a surprisingly effective instigator; "If these people could succeed in the luxury real estate market", I thought, "I could kick ass". If nothing else, getting a license would ensure I would never have to cede control to an incompetent agent ever again — and that was all the motivation I needed. I studied hard, passed the test, and achieved the status of a licensed real estate agent in the state of California. But I wasn't just starting in your average California town: I was starting in Silicon Valley. Underneath the veneer of peaceful suburbia lay one of the most expensive and competitive housing markets in the entire United States. It was out of the frying pan into the fire, but I was ready to cook.

As a new agent in a new town with few connections and no reputation, I was up against seemingly insurmountable odds — luckily, I was willing to put in the man hours to spin those odds in my favor. I knew the only way I would succeed in this cutthroat environment was to become obsessed with the work, to never be truly off the clock, and to be more disciplined than all of my competition. I started work early and rarely left before seven. I made every call a priority, always ready in case my cell started ringing. I networked with every individual possible, befriended all of my clients, and never let a Bar Mitzvah, birthday, or wedding go by unattended. I would work with people and build relationships around every house I sold — I would garner not just clients, but friends who would stay in my life forever. And throughout it all I kept a positive attitude and refused to become deterred, constantly reminding myself "nothing worthwhile is easy". Piece by piece, I established myself in Silicon Valley — and though I expected my career to grow, I did not anticipate the dream situation I had set myself up for. I was a great saleswoman with heat in the right place at the right time: selling million dollar listings at ground zero of the modern tech revolution. My good situation suddenly became a once in a lifetime opportunity. Though I had clients of many different stripes, I had more than a few that developed apps, were social media rock stars, or proudly wore the nerd-genius cliche stereotypical of someone buying a million dollar house in Facebook founder Mark Zuckerman's zip code. As Silicon Valley grew, so too did my my income, confidence, and love for my profession; culminating in my sale of the most expensive single family home in the United States. I have since left the Bay Area, but I will never forget the myriad listings, amazing relationships, and impressive career I achieved as the tech capital was securing its identity. Silicon Valley and I didn't just have similar stories — we helped each other write them.

The Secrets

1. Think Positively, and Keep At It

Many up and coming salespeople have asked me

what the "secrets" to being a great salesperson are, or if there's any sort of code that can be cracked. Unfortunately, there is not — but there are a few simple philosophies I stand by that I believe have allowed me to endure in an often harsh industry. My first philosophy: if things aren't working for you, keep working hard and persevere. So many agents get so discouraged so quickly — the most bountiful period of my life, June of 2011, was also the period I was seeing numerous agents drop like flies. I heard every excuse — "the market is awful!" "the economy is in the pits!" "nobody is buying!" and it would have been all too easy to join the chorus. But I believed in my ability to transcend my circumstance, and refused to join the pity party. And guess what? The discouraging market became a boon for me — my competition shrank, my profile grew, and I turned around and sold the first single family home in the United States for over $100 million.

Negative energy is contagious — not only is it tough to go to bat for the things that you love, but people would much rather read a bad review of a movie than a good review. Peer pressure is a menace — people on the way down will often want to take you with them, which is why it is important to maintain a positive attitude to maintain success. What I have found that with any degree of success, there are a lot of critics. Gain any degree of notoriety and you will find a hundred onlookers poking holes in your positive attitude, cynics telling you why you are wrong to shoot for the stars. These are actions of insecure, bitter individuals who attempt to build themselves up by knocking you down. I only bring this up as a warning: I know from personal experience just how easy it is to be discouraged by negative personalities (or even worse, to start thinking like them). When things seem most bleak and you are met with a chorus of naysayers – do everything in your power to reject negative sentiment and continue thinking positively. This is an important element of my philosophy on perseverance; pursue your goals without an ounce of bitterness. Perseverance is not about hanging around, feeling sorry for yourself — perseverance is about facing every day knowing you are going to win. Negative energy is contagious, but positive energy yields positive results.

I cannot emphasize the degree to which positive thinking has shaped my professional life. I remember in one of my first training classes before I even got my license, the teacher went around the room and asked everyone "how much are you going to make in your first year?". Most people shot low, I frequently heard "$50,000;" the dreamers went as high as "$100,000". When the question got around to me, I answered "I would like to make "$600,000". I got snickers, some laughs, and was primarily met with condescension. Could I have let this deter me, and let the people I was in the class with make me reconsider my dreams? It would have been all too easy, but I snapped out of it — who were these people, anyway? These people weren't my betters, we were in the same class! They literally knew just as much about real estate as I did! I looked past the facade of superiority that condescension creates, and proved their snickers wrong by making $400,000 my first year. I resolved to never let outside forces dictate my performance — if you don't believe in yourself, nobody else will. Love yourself immensely, and you will attract love. Treat all the people you work with (whether they be other brokers, vendors, or clients) with respect and integrity, and you will be rewarded with good reputation. Think positively, keep working, and treat even your harshest critics with respect; these are principles that are not only good for business, they are good for the soul.

2. Love What You Do.

"Love what you do, and you will never work a day in your life". This may be a cliche, but the truth behind it is immense. Love what you do. That, simply, is the secret to success and the second part of my philosophy. Why have I had more success in Real Estate than any other field? One can credit my work ethic — and I often do — but what has helped me ascend above and beyond your run of the mill agent is my authentic love of houses. To me, a beautiful house is more breathtaking than anything at the MoMA, as escapist as classic cinema. Properties that some might see as mediocre, I often see as the ultimate Cinderella story.

To me, there is no greater satisfaction than finding an average house and finding the right buyer; a prince for the shunned step sister. Anyone can sell a gorgeous house, it was my love for the unwanted orphans that made me stick out, selling properties that had been on the market for over a year. I was recently inspired by actor Jim Carrey's commencement address to Maharishi University of Management's class of 2014. Carrey told a story of his father who made a "conservative choice" in his career, taking a job as an accountant. "When I was twelve years old, he was let go", Carrey declares, "you can fail at doing something you don't want. So you might as well take a chance on doing something you love". If you do not share my sincere passion, obsession, and fascination for being a real estate agent, I advise you follow a different career path. No matter how great you are, you will feel a time when you're "just not there, just not getting it"; and you can allow that insecurity to take over you, or you can utilize your love for the work to power through that slump. Read negotiation books, listen to podcasts, know your market; prove that you love what you do. If you want to sell a $100,000 property, you should know everything about it. Your consistent effort to know everything and better yourself will allow you to become a true champion for your clients. If any of this discourages you from the job, you were probably not meant for it in the first place. The best real estate agents are the ones you could never talk out of doing it, and to them I say: welcome to the club.

3. Live a Life Worth Advertising

My final piece of advice: live a life outside of real estate. This is an easy one to dismiss, but striking a proper work/life balance took more trial and error than any other element of my career. When you are obsessed with work, the first person it's hard to make time for is yourself. If you are committed to the difficulty, time, and perseverance necessary to being a great real estate agent, you face the danger of succumbing to a life of endless work. Workaholism sounds glamorous, but like everything else in life, you need balance. Real Estate is a uniquely social industry, and consuming culture purely through the context of real estate is a surefire way to inhibit social interaction. Spending all weekend at the office can do a real number on your Sunday morning charm. Go on a hike before that open house and I guarantee you will exude more personality than if you spent the morning looking through escrow documents. Before you sell a house, you have to sell yourself — and if you want to charm, you better have more things to talk about than real estate. The most rewarding part of my real estate career was the bond I shared with my clients. I became friends with the people I worked with, which turned my work into my life instead of vice versa. But I wouldn't have held on to a single one of them if they never connected with me as an honest to goodness human being. Live a life worth advertising; go to the movies, read a book, go to the gym. Read up on that

TV show everyone's talking about, play with your kids, watch the news — all of this will make you more interesting and add dimension to your conversations.

If you take care of yourself physically and enrich yourself mentally, you will be more attractive to everyone you meet. When I moved to Los Angeles, I immediately sought to join the Los Angeles Opera — an organization I now operate on the board of. We currently serve the Los Angeles artistic community and, most importantly, offer 175,000 kids exposure to opera and music education. I am also a member of Women in Film as well as Film Independent, two organizations devoted the raising the profile of under-represented voices in film. I joined these organizations because I emphatically believe in giving back to my country, community, and planet — I would be literally nowhere without them. What made me a good agent was my affinity for the work, but what has made me a great agent is my life outside of real estate. Living a well-rounded life is what builds your personality, what makes you appear as more than a snake oil salesman. Though I found immense success in real estate, none of my hard work, persistence, or dedication would mean anything if I did not feel like a well-rounded person.

ABOUT THE AUTHOR: *Catherine Marcus*

Though my success in real estate may seem lucrative, it did not come without a grand amount of effort, positive thinking, and hard lessons learned. I made a lot of sacrifice, endured a lot of negative emotion, and faced many moments of doubt; but I endured by remembering that nothing worthwhile is easy, and that persistence is everything. Every struggle I encountered in the beginning were seeds to be harvested a decade down the line, the foundation on which I would sell the single most expensive single family home in the United States. After that sale, I finally was lucky enough to move back to Los Angeles, now working every day in Sotheby's beautiful Beverly Hills offices. And as I reflect on my intense, crazy journey I realize more than ever that my journey that has yet to end. I still live my dream. I still achieve success. But most importantly, I make the time to love every second of it. You can find me at www.CatherineMarcus.com.

Chapter 4

JEM: A Diamond in the Rough

The Creation of a Niche Market

By Jennifer Meehan

Chicago, Illinois

My child said, "We should have a hot cocoa stand in the winter, and then we can do hot apple cider the next time. . . I think we'd make a lot of money." This was the first time I saw the positive impact of my struggle as a single parent with no financial support on my little girl. My fancy financing and inability to let the challenge of having a baby on my own drove me to measures I didn't even know I had within. I had ALWAYS thought at the age of 35 I would be living in an affluent suburb with four kids; a stay-at-home mom, with my daily worry being what to make for dinner. However, my reality ended up the antithesis of this scenario. Fast forward and now I have become an agent to athletes worldwide.

I am sure you might love to hear about all of the professional athletes and celebrities I have worked with. Who is the hottest, who was the richest, who's place was most expensive and you might really even like to know the address. However, the cornerstone of JEM Luxury is to create an environment of total anonymity, to assure negotiations are not tainted. It is very easy for a seller to go on www.mlb.com and find out the salary of the pitcher for the Cubs or the salary for the Blackhawks re-signed goalie. JEM has an attorney on the team that covers the business on every angle to keep our confidentiality. So I am going to tell you instead how and why I created the boutique firm that now serves Chicagoland's most elite clientele.

I had gone to school overseas for my undergraduate education; I was bilingual, beautiful, and 100 percent fun. I sold one diamond earring to pay for my real estate class and the other for the exam. I worked on the trading floor at the Mercantile Exchange during the day and was a hostess at a small Italian restaurant in the evenings. The first condo I sold was $850,000 to a trader I was dating at the time. Then I gave really good phone on floor time and landed a New Jersey client who bought over $3 million in speculation condos, and I did open houses EVERY weekend from 11 a.m. to 1 p.m. and 1:30 p.m. to 3:30 p.m.

As I am writing this I need to be truthful and mention many of my Sunday Open Houses were actually reading the paper and nursing a hangover. But, it's all about creating opportunity on this business and BEING THERE…simply just being there. Once someone told me you get out what you put in and on a job paid fully by commission that phrase should never escape you.

In 2008, the real estate landscape changed. There were no more floor calls, open houses were too dangerous - after a fellow agent was attacked on a second showing in her listing off Burling, and on May 22, 2008 I had a baby girl, Marielle. I was unwed, left her dad when I was six months pregnant, and I was scared to death. I was literally paralyzed with fear.

I had a tough few years at that time in court battles getting full custody of my daughter. I had enough wits at the time to not let my license lapse, and although I didn't really "work" full time during that period of my life, I was still a Realtor®. And, being a Realtor® is what inevitably allowed me freedom from dating those people who weren't right for me, just as starting JEM allowed me freedom from paying a commission to a brand that wasn't right for me.

Now, what was going to be my next step? I was in an office again, same place different name; I don't mean this figuratively, but working in a large brokerage did not appeal to me. With the real estate market not being what it previously was, I started to panic.

This was an entirely different arena. . . or was it? Was it just that I had lost my confidence or sparkle because I had taken two years off? How am I going to support this little girl at home? How do you get business anymore? That's when it came to me to start a Sports Relocation Company. . . Chicago features four pro teams, the players are always in turnover, it was perfect!

I have always been a huge sports fan, especially hockey and baseball. Hockey because I live in Chicago, and the national anthem is spiritual at the United Center, with the dark gloomy days, it's always a good excuse to put on a cute outfit, some makeup, and catch a game. Baseball, because Wrigley field is another icon that holds nostalgia of being there as a child with my dad, sunshine, and a cool breeze from Lake Michigan on a hot day.

After a couple big sales, I bought (at the time) Harris Club tickets at the United Center. . . it's an uber cool level with open bar, a phenomenal food spread from filet to hot dogs, never ending desert table, pool table, you name it. When the Bulls were playing, the Black-hawks would be up there watching the game and vice versa, it was at the Harris Club where my social relationship with the players began. Through repetitive introduction, I soon began to be known as Jen the Realtor® and when I started JEM all I had to do was associate my name with my brand.

Team players are just that. . .team players. The majority of big time pro athletes have a philanthropic foundation that is typically annual and entails some type
of huge party. I began sponsoring one player and/or
manager from each sports team and have consistently
donated and raised funds. I realized that in return I
was not only showing support for my client but also
becoming a soft sell for my real estate company. Team
players. . .I support them , they in turn refer me to their
friends and family for real estate sales.

The entire cornerstone of sales is building strong
relationships. Never take short cuts; they fill your
pockets with gold, then you go for a swim and sink
to the bottom. High end sales were particularly hard
to get into because people perceive inexperience until
you are in your mid 30s, even though I have been selling since I was 23. It also took saying no to a lot of
listings that would have been easy money, but I was
aware enough from observing others for years in the
big brokerage houses that the lower end market was
NOT where I wanted JEM to go.

When selling luxury real estate, all of the real estate
professionals have access to the same Multiple Listing
Service (MLS), and the same comps. But to succeed,
it takes integrity, honesty, confidentiality, and good
relationships. The difference my company provides

is that I have lifelong personal relationships and a life-time of living in Chicago. For example, I put an offer in on 999 Lake Shore Drive last month, the Penthouse unit, and it wasn't even for sale. I have the skills to penetrate areas of the market that other agents simply will not be able to access.

The focus on JEM is to provide an elite, confidential high caliber, real estate service to high profile athletes and CEO's of the professional teams. Professional sports teams do not operate like corporations, each is on their own verses the larger corporations that provide relocation services.

Professional athletes are on their own their when it comes to finding a home, they find a real estate agent through word of mouth and/or their traveling team secretary. This was brought to my attention through my social interaction with the players, and I knew then that JEM had found a strong niche in the market.

Selling to professional athletes is what catapulted me into the luxury market. The struggle has been that some people think I exclusively sell to the athletes, which is not true. I offer a service to any client that has the same luxury needs as the athletes do. The pitch of JEM is personalized service.

With JEM, there is no reporting to third parties, there is no huge staff with knowledge of the famous person's new addresses or financials. It's me, Jennifer Meehan, two agents that work under me, my assistant, and a gaggle of attorneys. That being said, I limit the number of clients I take on, and this is not qualified by a specific number, rather the amount of time that is needed for each specific deal. The goal of JEM is supreme customer service, and in my business plan that can only be achieved by individual attention to a client's needs.

None of my success could have been achieved if it wasn't for my friends and family that have supported me throughout the years. The yoyo financial rollercoaster of being in the real estate business is very wearing and it takes the pep talks from friends to move forward and the confidence my family has given me to keep on keeping on.

I feel my most confident and bright when I find a home for a client in another state, when I have reached out to my sphere of influence and find them a match of both personality of the Realtor® and their dream home. From my involvement in the National Football League, Major League Baseball, and National Hockey League, I have exposure to an array of real estate agents. My clients typically have a short two-month period from the time they contact me until the time they NEED to buy a house that is on average in 2013 in the neighborhood of $2.3 million dollars. Knowing which Realtor® is right for them is key in the effectiveness of their relocation. These are significant purchases, not only because of the high price of properties but because their family will be there, living there and for much of the year without them. This being said these sales need to be fluid and concisely what the buyer wants. . . This is 100 percent my favorite deal to do, because my clients are amazing at how smoothly things fall into place when they are matched with a Realtor® that fits them. I love my work!

ABOUT THE AUTHOR: *Jennifer Meehan*

Jennifer Meehan is the owner of JEM Luxury, LLC, a boutique real estate firm located in Chicago, Illinois. Born and raised in the suburbs, Jennifer has been an Illinois resident for a majority of her life, making her extremely knowledgeable about the city and its surrounding areas. When she was not residing in Illinois, Jennifer was getting her bachelor's degree from the American University of Paris and San Louis University in Madrid, where she became fluent in Spanish.

WHY REAL ESTATE?

WHY DID JENNIFER START JEM LUXURY, LLC?

WHAT SETS JEM LUXURY, LLC APART FROM OTHER BROKERAGES?

The uniqueness of JEM Luxury, LLC as a real estate brokerage can be demonstrated in two aspects: discreet and personal relationships. Jennifer works directly one on one with her clients - their information is kept highly confidential without the larger number of people involved in transactions in larger brokerages. Thus, she insures her clients' information is kept private. From working with many of Chicago's athletes, CEOs, and elite, Jennifer is remarkable at keeping all information regarding her clients' transactions discreet. Jennifer handles every single step of the buying and selling transaction- from showing properties to the accounting aspect, Jennifer handles it all. Her clients know that with any questions or comments, they can simply call her and find their answer instead of being transferred to other departments. Furthermore, JEM Luxury, LLC is also beneficial for out-of-state clients in that there is not a relocation department that charges additional fees. Jennifer handles everything directly. Because of this one-on-one relationship between Jennifer and her clients, they are able to connect at a deeper level. Jennifer is passionate about helping clients find exactly what they are looking for- not just finding them a three bedroom, one bathroom unit overlooking Lake Michigan, but also paying attention to the details such as millwork quality, kitchen appliance brand, and the like. Each and every transaction is tailored differently to each individual client. Once she becomes knowledgeable of a client's style, she will go the extra mile to preview homes before deciding if it is right to take her clients to see them.

Find Jennifer Meehan at www.JemLuxury.com.

Chapter 5

Selling Every Listing!
Explosive Luxury Marketing, Colorado Style

By Christine and Carl Battista

Denver, Colorado

W e refer to Colorado as a "move-to" state. It is a state that people move to from other parts of the country and the world. People come here for all sorts of reasons: Some love the climate and upbeat atmosphere, the opportunities for outdoor activities like hiking, skiing, rafting, biking, and horseback riding. Others appreciate the fact that Colorado has low taxes and a diverse economy that appeals to startups and entrepreneurs as well as established corporations.

When it comes to luxury real estate, Carl and I specialize in "Denver and Beyond." Whether a luxury homebuyer wants to wake up to a dazzling urban cityscape or to the sight of the sun rising over the majestic Rocky Mountains, they will find their dream home in Colorado.

Because of the area's rich, vibrant culture, nearly limitless recreation options, and breathtaking scenery, Denver practically sells itself. However, this does not mean that the market is immune to the unique challenges that accompany luxury home sales: Luxury homes typically take longer to sell than other types of properties. This is primarily due to the fact that when you are selling million-dollar plus homes, your pool of potential buyers is limited.

Using a combination of traditional and non-traditional marketing strategies and unique, "wow-factor" extras such as aerial tours, mini-movies, voice-overs and on-site champagne dinners, Carl and I ensure that our clients' listings reach buyers in all parts of the country – and the world.

Denver Success Story: Penthouse of the Pros with Hollywood Connections

One of our favorite success stories is about a magnificent penthouse located in Downtown Denver's Riverfront Tower. The owners loved the location – it afforded stunning panoramic views of the city lights and mountains, and it was within walking distance of iconic area attractions such as the Broncos Stadium, the Pepsi Center, Coors Field, Riverfront Park, LoDo, and all vibrant Downtown Denver has to offer. The property had just about everything you could want in a luxury condominium.

The one thing the penthouse didn't have though, was a yard for the owners' 10 grandchildren to play. They were aware that they were selling during one of the worst times in market history, but they were determined to move – and they were determined to sell their penthouse for more than any re-sale since way before the market crash, wanting in the range of $2.5 million dollars.

At the time, the market was flooded with similar properties and the average "Days on Market" for a luxury condo was 18 months or more. It was the worst market we had ever encountered. Three downtown appraisers told us the sellers' price was very unrealistic, if not ridiculous.

"Don't ask anything above $1.9 million, not in this market."

Carl and I were not daunted. We aren't scared away easily, and we reject the idea of "averages." Additionally we had a good feeling about the property; we had faith in our extensive, cutting-edge marketing strategies, superior negotiation expertise and our history of selling every listing. To us, this represented an exciting challenge, and we knew we could defy the statistics.

I should point out Carl and I have the utmost respect for appraisers. They are highly educated professionals. Through no fault of their own, there are inherent challenges with guidelines they must follow. We knew our clients would not settle for a price less than $2 million. We felt cautiously confident we could sell their penthouse in a record range of $2.5 million, but we would have to do some in-depth research first.

We spent days analyzing, viewing and studying every luxury condo on the market, including several that were under contract. When complete, we put together an in-depth analysis and portfolio comparing this property with all of the relevant properties in the marketplace.

From there, Carl and I launched a comprehensive marketing campaign to sell the penthouse, which included numerous components. Five primary components were:

1. Internet Marketing via luxury architectural photography, tours and movies. The Internet is often a home's first and only "showing". What buyers (and their agents) experience online must absolutely "wow" them, or they will move on. We include inset photos, captivating twilight photography, glide-through tours, and/or mini-movies. Additionally we capture the best of the home's surroundings and the area. Luxury marketing is all about selling Lifestyle.

2. Global Marketing: The U.S. is a global market and Colorado is no exception. We market locally, regionally, nationally and around the world, using a combination of digital, print and email to targeted international buyers. We also market to international luxury agents - many which we know personally. We attracted several interested international buyers for this home. We are members of Keller Williams Luxury International and KW's Global Property Specialist Division, which provides our sellers unsurpassed Global exposure and international marketing.

3. Target Marketing: It starts with your data base. Carl and I have an exceptional data base including relationships with professional athletes, high net worth clients and high profile individuals - and per-sonally target-market to our sphere. We also define the answer to this question: "Who are the most likely buyers for this property?" We specifically defined our buyer pool and devised a detailed strategy to market to these potential buyers. This included: Pro athletes, coaches, business owners, segments of the oil and gas industry and others.

4. Story-Focused campaign materials: The sellers told us their penthouse (a stone's throw from the Denver Broncos Stadium, the Pepsi Center and Coors Field) was also the interim home for many pro athletes. They lived with the pros. We had already named the home "Penthouse of the Pros" and developed its story. Just before we launched our productions, we learned more.

As it turned out, the penthouse and its immediate surroundings were the backdrop for a film starring Eddie Murphy. We immediately re-customized our marketing to include both the pro athlete and Hollywood stories. Suddenly, this was not only the "Penthouse of the Pros", it was also the penthouse used as a back-drop for the movie, "Imagine That."

5. An exclusive invitation-only evening presenting the Penthouse. For this event, we invited targeted buyers, VIP guests, luxury agents and luxury vendors. We spend thousands on catering, entertainment, valet parking, publicity and even a take-home gift for guests. This is an excellent way to generate a buzz, increase exposure and generate an offer.

The penthouse sold in 20 days for $2.45 million - cash buyers who paid close to list price. This was the highest downtown residential re-sale in years. Our clients were thrilled. They received the price they hoped for and purchased a home, complete with a yard for their grandchildren.

Why Colorado?

There are hundreds of reasons for luxury homebuyers to love Colorado. Here are just a few of our favorites:

• **Uplifting climate and consistent sunshine.** Colorado is mild in the summer and snow melts quickly in the winter. What's more, Colorado is not prone to natural disasters such as hurricanes, earthquakes, or frequent tornadoes.

• **A diverse economy and "business-friendly" atmosphere.** Colorado is a favorite with businesses, start-ups and entrepreneurs thanks to the state's low taxes and pro-business policies.

• **Limitless outdoor recreation.** Whether you love mountain vistas, hiking, skiing, rafting, biking, boating or climbing, you can enjoy it in Colorado.

• **Denver.** Denver is a young, vibrant city full of culture, parks, amazing food, art, premier entertainment, world-class beer, seven professional sports teams, and a diverse population of people from all over the country – and the world.

• **Low property taxes.** Property taxes are significantly lower here than many areas of the U.S.

The funny thing is, we received the offer before our scheduled event. A buyer had been "wowed" by our marketing and submitted an offer a week prior to the event. Even though the home was no longer available, we went ahead with the entertainment, food and event. This special evening included several other agents and their listings. The penthouse was more-or-less the cornerstone of the entire evening. It just didn't feel right to cancel on the other agents or their sellers.

We were delighted with how quickly the penthouse sold in one of the worst markets in history. Of course this is not the case with every sale. This is why Carl and I have developed several innovative marketing strategies and options when it comes to selling luxury properties.

Thinking Beyond the Internet: "Leave No Stone Unturned"

Once staged and "show-home" ready, I have already mentioned expert photography is crucial, together with quality productions, all connected to the property's own website - and I really can't stress this enough. Nearly all homebuyers begin their searches on the Internet. The pictures, tours and the property's website must motivate buyers to get out of their chair and into the home. These represent crucial steps, but they are not the only steps.

Carl and I have a passion for "leaving no stone unturned." Although the Internet and digital marketing are the cornerstone of each of our luxury listings,

Every Picture and Web Production Tells a Story

Whether you are selling a multi-million dollar estate or a modest starter home, the photography and tour production you use will make or break your listing. Here is how to make the most of your photos and web production:

• **Hire a seasoned photographer.** Spend the money on a photographer who specializes in luxury residential photography. The results are worth it and you owe it to your sellers.

• **If the weather is not right, reschedule.** A rainy day can make even the most spectacular property look dreary. If the weather is not cooperating, Carl and I reschedule. This often means paying the photographer or film maker to come out again. What if this was your home?

• **Think quality and quantity*.** More photos (25-30) result in greater hits/page views and increased time "spent" in your home – and the more likely buyers will begin to imagine themselves living there. *Note: with certain homes, "less" may mean "more" for your seller!

• **Ensure every photo caption includes the address.** Once your photos go viral, there is no telling where they will end up. If your caption does not contain the location, buyers may not know how to contact you or find the property.

• **Use mini-movies, tours, voice-overs and aerials on-line.** YouTube is the second largest Internet search engine- and it's a great tool for luxury marketing. We utilize various productions such as aerial "fly-over" movies, voice-overs, glide-through tours, and/or mini-movies of every home, estate and mountain property.

extraordinary marketing efforts go far beyond uploading photos, movies, creating a property's website and telling its story.

We believe it is our duty to present every option to our clients, for the successful sale of their home. In the confines of traditional sales when a home has not sold, many agents feel the only viable strategy is "price lowering". We do not to subscribe to this theory in luxury real estate.

Understand the no-reserve luxury auction platform. This is an excellent marketing option for some sellers. Auctions are commonplace abroad and becoming more so domestically. Per NAR, "A real estate auction is an innovative and effective method of selling real estate. It is an intense, accelerated marketing process involving the public sale of any property - most certainly including non-distressed - through open cry, competitive bidding."

In partnership with a stellar luxury auction firm, we implemented this innovative global marketing strategy for one of the largest, most magnificent private residences in America - over 60,000 square feet of indoor-outdoor living space!

As listing agents, we can utilize this global marketing and sales platform for certain homes. Here are some key differences between traditional sales and a no-reserve auction:

• Time-driven results typically in 60 days or less vs. may remain on the market for years.

• National and international marketing vs. minimal marketing and heavy or total reliance on an MLS system.

• Seller sets a definite time frame for buyers to take action vs. seller waiting for a buyer.

• An auction creates urgency and fear of loss; this springboards buyers to take decisive action vs. use of price reductions to try to create buyer interest.

• Maximizes the true market value of a property. No limit on upside potential vs. potential is limited by the asking price.

• Property sold as-is. Inspections and conditions of sale are done in advance, eliminating negotiations, vs. traditional sales where contingencies abound: The seller must negotiate all aspects of sale and are often forced to re-negotiate mid-stream, after a buyer's inspections.

• Carrying costs are eliminated due to timely sale vs. seller carrying costs that are incurred for months or years - draining away seller equity and their bottom line.

• Agent has help with comprehensive marketing at no additional cost to them, receives full commission, and normal market time is about 60 days or less.

The best luxury auction firms can help you give your client comprehensive exposure and momentum to reach your most qualified audience around the world. The key to create spirited and competitive bidding is to attract the best buyers. The most valuable commodities in the world such as art, automobiles and properties, are often sold through an auction platform.

Additional World Class marketing strategies include:

Target marketing. Know your market. Is the home on a lake, near a golf course or a sports arena? Who are your buyers? Look at the near-by amenities and the demographics. You can purchase lists of names for almost any category from a "list-house", a service specializing in retrieving specific information about people, companies, and organizations.

Carl and I use this information to send letters or brochures to potential buyers. Depending on the location, we may send brochures to members of a certain organization or audience.

We used this strategy to sell a residence located near a lake. We obtained names of people who owned boats within a seven-county area, and sent letters to this target audience. One couple who received this letter had just invested thousands of dollars remodeling their home. They had no intention of moving. When they read the letter though, they were intrigued: They were passionate about boating, and the idea of being near a lake appealed to them. They called us to schedule a showing, and they fell in love with the property. A few days later, they signed a contract for the home near the lake, and put their newly remodeled home on the market.

Carry mini-brochures. You never know when or where you are going to meet a potential buyer. This is why Carl and I carry around miniature brochures for our luxury listings. These are small enough to fit in a pocket or purse. We have given them out on the ski slopes, at grocery stores and almost anywhere you can think of.

Reach out to luxury retailers and service providers. Think luxury car dealers, upscale hotels and more. When we take on the responsibly of marketing and selling another's home, we reach out and hand-deliver brochures to luxury vendors, hotels and more.

This strategy has worked for us: For example, one concierge ended up talking with a guest from the mountains who came to Denver often on business. As the CEO of a high-tech ski equipment firm, he was tired of staying in hotels and made an offhand comment about finding a place in town. The concierge slipped him a brochure for one of our luxury condos.

The CEO scheduled a property tour and signed contract a few days later. It just goes to show that you never know where your next buyer will come from.

We personalize the sales process. Before showings, Carl and I find out as much about the potential buyers as possible, and create a portfolio tailored to them. In addition to including details about the home, we share information about the local area, Colorado and more.

Unless a buyer absolutely says "No" to a property, we may invite them to experience the home again. This could include a champagne tour with Hors D'oeuvres, candles, music, a decadent dessert, and-or a secret surprise. This gives buyers a chance to feel at home and emotionally "move in." Optionally, we can send them away with a small marketing gift also. We find that if we can get a buyer to this point, we can almost always count on a "win" for the seller.

The most important aspect about Luxury Home Selling Mastery is this: It's all about serving others, not just in real estate but in life. When you focus on others, you will attract success!

ABOUT THE AUTHORS:
Christine and Carl Battista

Before I became a REALTOR®, Certified Luxury Home Marketing Specialist CLHMS), and successful real estate Investor, I was (and still am) an ICU nurse. It was not an easy job, but it was fulfilling and inspirational. In dying, my patients taught me how to live.

They helped me realize what matters in life. What matters is relationships – with one another and our Creator, and doing the right thing.

My husband Carl and I bought and sold investment properties for several years before we made the decision to become real estate professionals. Carl and I have sold millions and millions of dollars' worth of real estate, but it's about others, not money, recognition or rewards.

We consistently deliver World Class concierge services, unparalleled negotiating and explosive marketing. We care for clients just like our family. We spend the time and resources to market every property as if it were our own. And, we thrive on pricing aggressively! It is a great responsibility and honor, as our homes are normally the largest investments people make in their lives.

Carl has also earned the CLHMS-Certified Luxury Home Marketing Specialist. He was a finance director for Fortune 100 companies and started investing in real estate at 16 years old. Carl's negotiation, contract and finance background coupled with highly successful property investment expertise, makes him uniquely qualified for successful negotiations. My background in business and critical care has uniquely vetted me for stellar marketing, negotiating, caring for and fiercely protecting our clients. We view ourselves as "servant-leaders" in the industry. We're passionate about helping our clients, in any way we can. We have facilitated everything from staging, to temporary housing, to lawn mowing. We've chartered planes and other devices to take aerial movies and photos of clients' properties. No job is too small or too large for our world class team.

Perhaps unsurprisingly, our other passion is Colorado. I especially love introducing clients to the beauty and wonder of our home state – probably because I am not a native. I am, like so many others here, a Coloradan by choice. I grew up hundreds of miles away, in Michigan, which has a lot to offer, when the weather cooperates. I knew early on I wanted to go somewhere sunny. My father raved about Colorado's beauty. He traveled there a few times for medical conventions, and he always came home with stories of amazing blue skies and breathtaking mountain vistas.

I suppose that's why I left Michigan for Colorado right after college. My roommate at the time moved with me. We had college degrees in nursing and business and decided to present ourselves to area hospitals as a "package deal." Neither of us had set foot in Colorado before – but as soon as we arrived and saw the Rocky Mountains set against that brilliant blue sky, we knew we were home!

Now, nearly two decades later, I still wake up every morning feeling energized and uplifted by the sight of that blue sky. Colorado is a beautiful, magical place. Every day is a sunrise. I simply can't imagine living anywhere else.

Carl and I love Colorado and we love real estate – but to us, the most important things about our profession are making a difference and results. We continue to earn various top industry honors: In addition to the CLHMS status, we have been inducted into the coveted Institute For Luxury Home Marketing's Million Dollar Guild, earned membership in Keller Williams Luxury International, and are Global Property Specialists. Consistently we are awarded the Five-Star Professional Award, as seen in 5280 Magazine. Subsequently we have been asked to speak on Luxury Marketing at local, regional and nation venues including the Global Property Specialist retreat and "Leaders in Luxury", an invitation-only event for top luxury agents in North America.

Our sales track record along with the Five-Star Award, are the most meaningful. This is from a completely independent company, based on anonymous, comprehensive client satisfaction and feedback surveys covering dozens of areas from results, to integrity and negotiation skills. It is awarded only to the top percent in the region. To us, this is confirmation our passionate dedication, caring and world class real estate services are helping to make a difference in the lives of others. In the end, this is what matters the most.

Christine & Carl Battista, The Battista Team
Keller Williams DTC Luxury International
Christine: Christine@TheBattistaTeam.com
Carl: Carl@TheBattistaTeam.com
TheBattistaTeam.com
303-771-7500

Chapter 6

Why the WORLD Adores Miami

By Brigitte Lombari and Richard Lombari

Miami, Florida

There are few cities in the world that can boast of great year-round weather, incredible bright, fine, sandy beaches, dynamic dining, music and nightlife energy, where diverse ethnic cultures all meld together in a unique world class living experience as they do in Miami.

This is why the WORLD Adores Miami!

Hyperbole? Not at all. The statement is backed by verifiable facts. More than 14 million people visited Miami last year, with over half of them arriving from other countries. Miami's visitors ADORE Miami so much that 70 percent are returning!

The world's spotlight has often turned to Miami...You may remember the opening scene of the 1964 movie Goldfinger, as the viewer flies over Miami Beach to the famous Fontainebleau Hotel where James Bond is lounging by the pool while enjoying a friendly massage. In the 1980s, it was the cool tropical style of undercover detectives Crocket and Tubbs in Miami Vice that helped build the city's fun beach party reputation and tourist base. And it was Will Smith's 1997 recording hit "Miami" that once again turned eyes to South Beach.

According to a recent study*, Miami ranked #7 in the luxury real estate market in the WORLD and #4 in the United States. The study included a range of factors including the number of sales over $1M, growth in luxury market sales, and record sales prices. The study also found that by comparison, Miami's luxury real estate is inexpensive: it is the lowest-priced city of the top 10 rated in price per square foot for luxury homes. Combine this outstanding luxury value, the amazing culture and lifestyle with the lack of a state income tax, Miami becomes a magnet for the wealthy.

This magnet theory is easily evident by the extensive list of sports superstars, TV, movie and recording stars that called Miami home. From the sports world, basketball superstars Pat Riley, Dwayne Wade, Chris Bosch and LeBron James have built nests here as has baseball Legend Alex Rodrigues from the New

York Yankees. The list goes on…Actors Matt Damon, Dwayne "The Rock" Johnson and Sylvester Stallone. Recording artists: Lenny Kravitz, Madonna, Shakira, Jennifer Lopez, John Secada and Grammy winning rapper Pitbull, "Mr. Worldwide" who was previously known as Mr. 305 for the Miami area code he grew up in.

The overwhelming luxury residential product of choice for locals and international clientele alike are beachfront condominiums. The gleaming towers of chic elegance draw the uber-wealthy with new construction prices starting in the $4 Million range. At the top end, priced at an eye popping $55 million is a 15,000 sq ft penthouse at the Mansions at Acqualina. The six-bedroom, eight-bathroom unit includes a 5,000-square-foot terrace, a theater, private elevator, wine room, billiard room, an indoor pool and a "sky garden" with 30-foot ceilings, a waterfall, and a cantilever glass pool overlooking the ocean.

In addition to amazing ocean views, private elevators, 24-hour valet, security and concierge services, multiple pools, hot tubs, professional quality gyms, party and game rooms and theaters, nearly all luxury condos offer full service beach amenities, including private cabanas, umbrellas, lounge chairs, towels, and food and beverage service.

More internationally recognized hotel brands have

joined the latest luxury condo wave. The permanent residences often benefit from requisite hotel guest amenities like onsite spas and gourmet restaurants. Recent branded additions to the Miami Luxury condo boom include St. Regis Resort and Residences; W South Beach, The Residences and several towers with Trump branding. Currently in the initial sales phase are the Ritz-Carlton Residences and the Surf Club Four Seasons Private Residences.

With so much competition for the world's wealthiest buyers, condominium developers are elbowing each other with super amenities to wrestle attention to their project. Consider the elaborate Porsche Design Tower in Miami that features three-car elevators that whisk you and your car directly to your unit! At Echo Aventura, in addition to smart building technologies and complementary dog-walking service, all penthouses feature their own private plunge pools. A new boutique condo project, "O" Residences provides free on-call boats for their residents.

However, not all of Miami's high net worth individuals live in posh condos. Many prefer to live on an estate on the ocean, the bay, a canal or on one of the several exclusive man made islands in Miami's intracoastal waterways.

Boating is a major driver of the Miami luxury market. Last year, one of our clients brought their captain on board to "make or break" the deal. The home inspection was scheduled for the day of their return from the island of Bimini, so the captain could verify the ease of navigation to the home. The captain quickly docked and with a thumbs up and a big smile, the deal was all but done!

Of Miami's islands, perhaps the most desirable is a tiny guard gated island aptly named Star Island. Residents on this island of just 34 waterfront lots have included comedian Rosie O'Donnell, Musicians Gloria Estefan, Sean Combs, Julio Iglesias and Enrique Iglesias, Actor Don Johnson and NBA Champion Shaquille O'Neal. Asking prices for homes on the island average over $25 million.

Another beautifully landscaped and maintained high security island is La Gorce. This guard gated, patrolled neighborhood has been home to celebrities Cher, Billy Joel and Lil Wayne. A recent sale on the island hit the $30M mark. The neighboring La Gorce Country Club is a Jack Nicklaus-designed golf course with a 50,000-square-foot clubhouse. The exclusive, invitation-only membership initiation fee for equity "Founder" member is $80,000. If you have the friends to sponsor you, and the cash to purchase membership, be prepared to wait. The club maintains a waiting list.

Even a bit more secluded, with access only via car, ferry or private boat, is the privately owned Fisher

Island. Owners on the Island are in wealthy company. CNN Money has named Fisher Island the No. 1 Zip Code for income. And it's not surprising, just joining the Fisher Island Club requires an initial contribution of $250,000 with annual dues of $18,000. Amenities include pristine beaches, golf course, tennis courts, marina, pools, luxurious spa and wellness center, restaurants and lounges.

Much of Miami's current flow of luxury real estate growth has been fueled by an international appetite. Our foreign friends don't just visit. They BUY... and BUY BIG; and 90 percent of them purchase with CASH! The country taking the top slot for investment in Miami varies from year to year due to exchange rate fluctuations, homeland economic growth, or financial or political instability.

Last year 69 percent of all international sales in Miami were derived from the Latin American Caribbean region. Leading the list was Venezuela, Argentina, Brazil and Peru, representing a combined 52 percent of all international sales in Miami.

In Miami, any transaction may become a truly international affair. Last year we listed a Miami (North America) condo owned by a Netherlander (Europe) married to a Peruvian (South America). When the offer came in from a Russian real estate agent representing a Kazakhstani, I was in France visiting my in-laws while the seller was in Qatar (Asia). This single transaction had fingers in seven countries and four continents! Thank goodness for Skype, DHL, email and the ability to wire funds!

I'm not exaggerating a bit. In the Miami market it is crucial to have at your fingertips the tools, systems and team to perform luxury internationally. The first and most important step is educating foreign clients about the real estate process in the US and more specifically in Miami. Real estate is very different in other countries. Many international consumers expect that to see all the properties that might match their needs, they have to work with multiple agents as they do in their home country. A great consultation should explain how real estate agents receive compensation; plus can assist them in finding the right new construction home or condo and the flow of the entire transaction. Provide the BIG picture and then if they don't already have their own trusted professionals, introduce the potential clients to partner professionals: immigration attorneys, tax attorneys, translation services, multi-lingual staff and sales team.

As in any transaction, regardless of the price point, a real estate agent's job is to make EVERYONE's job easier.

When working with a buyer, help the co-operating agent help the seller make an easy decision to select your clients offer. Think of each offer as a court case, provide an abundance of supporting documentation. Provide information about the pricing, information about the buyer's motivation and ability to purchase.

When working with the seller, the process of making the job easier for the co-operating agent and the eventual buyer starts long before either has been identified. Agents should have multilingual e-flyers and websites and belong to various international real estate portals greatly increasing international exposure. Lots of high quality pictures and videos are needed because often the search begins even before the buyer lands in the United States.

Even though these tips are important in all transactions, it is even more essential in an international transaction with natural barriers of different languages, cultures and customs. The sooner these barriers are lowered the greater the odds of a successful transaction.

Consider your communication tools: As I mentioned earlier, communicating via internet video conference is excellent. Last week one of our team showed a brand new listing to his client in France via Skype. He was with them live videoing from his phone room by room and answered their questions. They placed an offer on the unit without ever stepping foot inside!

Google Hangouts is an online chat accessible within Gmail or on your phone. When working late, or early, I may catch clients available in other time zones at times I would never call them, for a quick information exchange.

For communicating via phone or text message internationally, we often use the smart phone app Viber. Operating over either Wifi or Cell phone internet service, calling with Viber is spooky clear!

Personally, I don't suggest Google Translate for websites or substantial in-depth communication. There really is too much risk. I do however, use Google Translate for short emails I receive to route them to the right person on my team.

There are many other MUST DO's in mastering Miami luxury real estate, though I think they are generally universal for any market to develop credibility and referability:

• What you wear matters: Luxury consumers know luxury products. They notice.

• What you drive matters

• Who you associate with matters: Refer only top quality people and resources.

• What you know matters: Most luxury consumers are extremely well-educated and experienced. Don't fake knowledge. Study the macro markets, micro markets and individual properties and it is really important to know materials, styles and trends.

Opportunity is everywhere as the Miami luxury market thrives. Whether it is the weather, the beaches, world class shopping, the boat, art or fashion shows, Miami is attracting multimillionaires from the Northern US and Canada and around the entire globe like never before!   There is one undeniable fact... The WORLD ADORES Miami!

*2014 report by Christies International Real Estate entitled: Luxury Defined: An Insight into the Luxury Residential Property Market

---

ABOUT THE AUTHORS:
Brigitte Lombari and Richard Lombari

Brigitte Lombari

Brigitte, originally from Paris, France focused her studies on Marketing and Human Resources and received a Master's Degree from the University of Paris. Her innovative marketing ideas and negotiating savvy with a myriad

of vendors led her to great success as project manager in the largest advertising Company in Europe (Publicis).

Since moving to Miami in 2004, Brigitte has been applying these advanced people and marketing skills to the real estate world with incredible success which is evidenced by the fact she has been consistently recognized as a top Realtor® with massive sales volumes placing her in the top 3 percent of all Realtors® nationally.

Luxury and international clientele particularly appreciate Brigitte's enthusiastic commitment to providing high quality, professional, and personalized services with emphasis on reliability and timeliness.   Her advanced knowledge of immigration and real estate law, local economies and customs coupled with her extensive internet focused marketing strategy (Domestic and European website exposure, high quality marketing materials, highly detailed custom brochures, social media and e-flyers as well as streaming video presentations...) literally attracts clients from around the globe.

Noting that individuals of high net worth have significant investment needs, Brigitte has successfully added commercial real estate to her repertoire. Her recent impressive commercial deals have included multiple bulk condo sales in Aventura and Midtown Miami, and multi-family deals in Hallandale and Miami Beach. Brigitte represented the buyer of the iconic Cavalier Hotel on Ocean Drive in South Beach. In 2014, Brigitte was awarded the prestigious title of Director of KW Commercial, a division of Keller Williams Elite Properties.

In 2012, with her husband Rich, Brigitte launched the IAdoreMiami Group which in just two years, currently ranks #26th in the state of Florida and #322 in the entire USA, of the more than 100,000 agents in Keller Williams Realty.

Rich Lombari

Rich has consistently implemented a methodical approach to developing sales teams that produce raving fans, referrals, exponential production growth and profitability. The combination of training, skills and accountability, has his teams reach their individual peak performance and attain their personal financial goals. Rich has spoken nationally for real estate industry professional organizations including the Council of Residential Specialists and the Women's Council of Realtors® and various national franchise real estate brokerages around the country.

Rich is a 24-year real estate veteran who has progressed from REO Sales to Corporate Relocation to specializing in the luxury home market for the last 15 years. Rich served as the Market Center Team Leader for two Keller Williams Realty offices, launching each into massive profitability and earning recognition as the Top Team Leader in his region.

Rich currently holds Real Estate Broker's Licenses in both California and Florida and is a Certified Residential Specialist (CRS), a Graduate of the Realtor® Institute (GRI), earned the prestigious designation of Certified Luxury Home Marketing Specialist (CLHMS) and was inducted into the Million Dollar Guild of the Institute of Luxury Home Marketing.

You can find the Lombaris at www.IAdoreMiami.com.

Chapter 7

Three Reasons Your Luxury Home Isn't Selling

By Wade Hanson

Twin Cities, Minnesota

Price. Accurately pricing your luxury home can be difficult and is more important now than ever before. If there is one thing I have learned in more than 15 years of working with wealthy buyers, this is it. You cannot sell a wealthy homebuyer a one-dollar bill for five bucks. These buyers are able to purchase the finer things in life due to the solid, informed monetary decisions they have made, and they aren't about to be duped into buying a home for more than it is worth. As a seller and an agent in the luxury market it's important to understand that no two luxury homes are alike, so attempting to find "comparable" sales can be very challenging and often times impossible. Some of the factors that need to be considered when pricing a high-end home are:

• Relevant properties that have sold in the last year.

• What features did the relevant home sales have that might be similar to the home you are selling?

• What was the average dollar per square foot sale price of those homes that recently sold?

• What is the average sale price compared to the tax-assessed value of the high-end home sales in the area?

• Maybe most important factor is; what was the actual number of real buyers that moved through the market compared to the number of homes that were available? This is referred to as the absorption rate.

Gone are the days of "let's try it at this price and see what happens". If your home is not accurately priced when it first hits the market, agents and buyers will overlook it. With the rising inventory of new listings and stiff competition, luxury buyers and agents simply will not waste their time looking at a home with an unrealistic seller. Many sellers will ask me "Why don't buyers just make me an offer? I am willing to negotiate." Luxury buyers are busy professionals and their time is valuable, they will not waste it looking at an overpriced home - period. If they do look at your home, and consider it overpriced, often times your home is used to help sell a more reasonably priced home because then that home will look like a tremendous value compared to yours. If you think you can drop the price in 60 days if it doesn't sell, and still get top-dollar for your home, you're wrong. Your home will be "labeled" and buyers will wonder what is wrong with it. I can't tell you the number of times this has happened. Buyers see a home that has been on the market for months and they love everything about it but they can't overcome the mental hurdle of "why hasn't someone else purchased this home? Something must be wrong with it." Or they say – "if it's this difficult for them to sell, I don't want to be in the same position when I have to sell". Time on the market due to overpricing can end up costing sellers hundreds of thousands of dollars!

Condition - Buyers are more demanding today than ever before. This is due to the amount of homes they have to choose from, and in my market, the amount of newer construction luxury homes sellers have to compete with. It's important to note that when you have an older home that will be competing with newer construction, you will need to either make the necessary updates or price your home to meet the condition it is in. Kitchens, bathrooms and the main living areas should be the focus when making updates. Simple updates like paint, new flooring and updated light fixtures can separate your home from the competition. And don't forget the exterior, green grass, no weeds and a fresh pot of flowers sound simple but are often overlooked by the seller. Buyers often form an opinion of your home by looking at the photos online or in an advertisement, then driving by the exterior to check out the curb appeal and the neighborhood. If it looks poorly maintained or like a lot of work to them, you've lost the buyer before they will ever consider looking. Often sellers will ask if they can offer an allowance to a buyer to make the necessary updates and then price the home like the updates have already been completed. In my opinion this is one of the worst incentives a seller can offer. Either do the work or price it accordingly! An allowance says to a buyer – this is a fixer-upper and buyers will expect a discount if they have to go through the hassle of doing the work themselves.

Don't forget to work with a professional interior designer to stage your home. In my experience, staging will add an additional four to six percent to the sale price. A good agent should have an interior designer that specializes in luxury homes to help with this process. I recently took on a listing that was 15 years old, owned by the original owners and everything in the home was original. The home had a dated kitchen with old cabinets and countertops, brass light fixtures and believe it or not - carpeting in the bathrooms! Against my recommendation, the seller tried to sell it without updating any of these areas and elected to price it as though it had been updated. They failed miserably. We had dozens of showings in the first 60 days and the comments were all consistent – the buyers could not look around the old kitchen and carpet in the bathrooms. We took it off the market for 60 days, remodeled the kitchen and bathrooms, put it back on the market and it sold in two weeks with fewer showings at a higher price! Remodeling can be a headache, but if you follow your agents direction, it will pay off.

Agent - No – not all agents are created equal! Selecting an agent that not only specializes in luxury homes in your area but is also a full-time, professional agent with several years of experience marketing homes such as yours will make a huge difference to your bottom line. Selecting the right agent that fits the type of home you are selling is in my opinion, the most important decision a seller will make. The right agent can properly guide you on the appropriate price, the correct marketing strategy and the improvements you should make prior to putting your home on the market based on their knowledge of the market, the overall market conditions and the agents experience working with buyers and sellers in the luxury market. The relationship with your Realtor® is a professional partnership that should feel right and comfortable for both parties with an emphasis on respect for your time, priorities and goals. I see so many sellers go with a friend or relative that lacks the skills and expertise to market the type of home they are selling and later regret their decision. This doesn't mean your friends and relatives don't know the industry, but you need to understand the real estate industry is no different than a medical or legal profession – it takes specialization to be successful. A brain surgeon can't perform a heart transplant and a divorce attorney has no business defending a criminal, just like someone that specializes in downtown condo sales has no business selling a lakefront vacation home. Simply putting a sign in the yard, snapping a couple of photos with their phone and placing your home on the MLS will not get the job done.

I believe in the luxury market each home is unique and tells a story. That story then needs to be properly conveyed to the appropriate group of prospective buyers. Selling a luxury home requires the equivalent planning, positioning and market analysis as any luxury brand. You need an agent that will make your home stand out from the crowd with an aggressive marketing plan catered to buyers that are looking for homes such as yours. There may be dozens of new listings that come on the market every day similar to your home and a good agent will know how to separate your home from the others. I love having a competing listing for sale in the same neighborhood because I know that if a seller listens to my pricing and staging recommendations that my marketing strategy will make their home stand tall above the competition and ultimately the competition will help to sell my listing.

Recently I had a seller come to me after having his home on the market for four years with four different Realtors®. All four real estate professionals were successful in their given marketplace – but this home was truly a one-of-a-kind luxury home and nothing like it had sold in the area in over 10 years. The previous four agents all took the same approach, with low quality photos, a sign in the yard and simply placing the home on the MLS waiting for a buyer. What they weren't focusing on was trying to determine who the buyer was and where they could be found. I took the listing and sold it in less than two weeks for 99 percent of the list price. How? Well it took some creativity, hard work and a huge investment on my part into marketing the home to the right buyers.

First, I needed to find out more about why the current owners purchased this home when they moved here from Italy 30 years ago. What did they like best about the home? What made them fall in love with this home? Their answer was simple – it wasn't so much the home itself but the location and the setting. They loved the views of the lake, the peaceful walking trails and the close distance to major amenities like downtown Minneapolis where they liked to frequent museums, festivals, the opera and orchestra concerts (not to mention it was only 15 minutes from the airport and they liked to travel). Now I had a story to tell. Next comes the challenging part (the part I love), the challenge of conveying this story to the correct audience. For this home, it started with fabulous photography of not only the home, but also the setting. The previous agents took a traditional photo from the street of the front of the home and frankly, this home didn't' have a ton of "curb appeal". The photos needed to tell this story of a peaceful setting. I instructed my photographer to focus on the rear of the home and the lake views. I was looking for one "money shot" that could convey to prospective buyers the feeling of being hundreds of miles away from the hustle and bustle of the city. For this we needed photos taken at different times of the day so we could capture the morning sun, the sunsets, as well as the beauty of this home at dusk. We also had the home professionally staged with a focal point on the piano room and the library with the hopes of attracting a buyer that had the same love of the arts as the sellers. You can't underestimate the power of photos; I believe that the photos are often times the most important piece of the marketing puzzle.

Once I had good photos in hand I needed a solid "multi-tier" marketing plan that would reach the right audience. Simply placing the home in the Multiple Listing Service and sticking a sign in the yard wouldn't get the job done as this home had been on the market for four years and was market worn and being overlooked by the local market. I started by creating a custom website that would allow me to put unlimited photos and information about the property for buyers to click through. This would really allow me to tell the entire story of this home to the audience. In addition to making sure the home was properly placed on the major real estate websites, highlighting the "story" we were telling and with a link to the website - I also believe there is still a need to advertise in print publications. Buying a luxury property is often more of a spur-of-the-moment inspiration than a long-planned purchase. Chances are you may not have been looking to acquire a new property when, out of the blue, a unique property presented itself and you found yourself envisioning owning it. This is when lifestyle magazines can be a useful marketing tool. The internet advertising and print publications were followed by rolling out the red carpet at a well planned public open house. Wait – open houses don't work in the luxury market right? The good news is this is what most Realtors® think when in reality, luxury buyers love the low pressure and convenience an open house has to offer.

And guess who purchased the home – a Professor at the University of Minnesota. The professor was relocating to the area, saw the ad in a lifestyle publication and visited the open house while there were dozens of other potential buyers there commenting on what a nice setting this home had and how difficult it is to find something like this. These buyers also wanted the same conveniences the sellers loved about the home – proximity to downtown and the airport. They were coming from Kansas City Missouri and had heard how beautiful the lakes of Minnesota were but didn't think they could find a setting like this close enough to the University of Minnesota, and to the things they liked to do on the weekends like attend opera and orchestra concerts!

If you can find the right agent that specializes in your market, he or she should be able to accurately price your home, highlight it's best features and most important – convey those features to prospective buyers. Selling a luxury home is an art and if price, condition and agent are all working together in harmony you will reap the highest possible price and your home will sell in the shortest amount of time.

ABOUT THE AUTHOR: *WADE HANSON*

Wade's real estate career began in 1999 and he quickly climbed to the top of the industry. By 2005 he had built an $80 million dollar, multi-office real estate firm and was named one of Realtor® Magazine's prestigious Top 30 Under 30 for top Realtors® in the country under the age of 30. Wade's dedication to client's needs, coupled with a passion for his business, formed a great foundation.

Wade is a Certified Luxury Home Marketing Specialist and a member of the prestigious Million Dollar Guild with The Institute for Luxury Home Marketing. This recognition is awarded only to those in the luxury home market who meet or exceed stringent performance standards and have specific upper-tier market knowledge.

Wade understands that marketing luxury properties is all about identifying the key characteristics that make a home unique, finding the home's story, and telling that story to the right prospects. The fact is, not all agents are equipped to handle a luxury property. Buyers and sellers in the upper-bracket demand more skill, knowledge and effort than the average agent is willing to provide a client.

Today, Wade remains one of the top real estate Brokers in Minnesota and Western Wisconsin representing luxury buyers and sellers. His early success story, drive and determination was key in being chosen as a contestant on Season 10 of NBC's The Apprentice – a reality TV series headed by real estate mogul and billionaire Donald Trump.

Wade's "no excuses" attitude and conviction that you have to live with the choices you make drive his engaging, competitive attitude. To learn more about Wade visit www.WadeHanson.com or contact him at wade@wadehanson.com or 651-274-8584.

Chapter 8

Luxury Home "Match Making" Using Today's Technology

By Liz Venema and DeAnna Armario

Pleasanton, California

Match Making with the iPad

In preparation for our luxury open houses, we download an App on our iPad called Open Home Pro. This iPad App is one of the most important tools we have found that has helped us sell many luxury homes and has brought us many luxury clients. It's the number one tool to our success with match-making the buyer to the home that we are promoting. We always remember many of our luxury clients are used to technology. They use it daily, signing into an iPad is normal to them; they like it because it is something that they know, something they are familiar with. The iPad is the tool of least resistance. We tailor the questions we want to ask our potential buyers beforehand. The great thing about this App is that we can download a picture of the home we are showcasing, we can tailor the questions to that home, and we can specify facts about the home, such as square footage, how many baths, bedrooms and any other highlights we want to add. That information along with the information from the potential buyer goes immediately into our data base. The buyer also will get a welcoming email from us, thanking them for visiting our open house, plus it will have the information about the open house (since many buyers visit multiple open houses on the same day). The iPad communication sets us a level above the rest!

Once the open house is complete, we contact the buyer from the information that they share with us. We ask them if they are interested in the home they visited. We ask about their thoughts on the home and then we take it from there.

We always ask the potential buyer if they are willing to receive a call from or future email from us. We don't want to step over that fine line of being annoying (nobody wants spam in their inbox) but we are interested in helping them secure their next home. Whether it is the one we are showing or we talk at a future time about what they are looking for. Some buyers know immediately that they want to purchase the home we selling, others wait. Having their information in our data base helps us easily access their information for negotiation whether they buy then or wait to buy later.

Global Match Making Luxury Homes

We met a husband and wife, originally from Hong Kong, at an open house we had listed for $2.49 million in Ruby Hill, located in the San Francisco East Bay Area. We greeted them and then asked them to sign into our iPad; we then gave them a private showing and walk through of the home. We talked about the home we were showing, finding out what their needs were such as price, square footage, do they need a loan? Do they have a lender? Are they a cash buyer? Have they lived in this area before? Where are they from? What brought them here today? We try to find a warm connection to the potential buyer, something we will remember about them and something they will remember about us. This couple could have chosen anyone to work with but they chose us and it all started with our iPad-our first point of contact and our confident approach.

The iPad App also works to enlist the buyer's agent that might be touring homes with the buyer. They always leave their business card but we like to have their information so that we can contact them immediately and ask what their client thought of the home and if they would like to move forward with purchasing it. The iPad gives us a paperless trail and puts all information into our data base for future conversations.

Match Making: Good Old-Fashioned Gift of Gab

We were holding an open house at one of our listings in Ruby Hill, a $2.25 million home. A woman came in and immediately said before I could produce my iPad, "I don't want to give my information; I just want to look around while my husband is watching the football game." She explained that she already lived in Ruby Hill. As we went up the stairs and I was pointing out all the plusses about the home, I was also asking her questions about her own life. As we talked I asked if she had children. Yes, she had three children and I asked about their schools. We started having a conversation about the teachers my girls had at the same school. It turned out these teachers from elementary school were also her children's teachers currently or at one time. We had our children's favorite teachers in common, which was a great start to any future conversations.

One of the teachers was Lynn Crawford, a fifth grade teacher and mother to Brandon Crawford, a shortstop for the San Francisco Giants baseball team. I told her a story about our family: I had run an elite childcare for many years that specialized in helping local teachers. All four Crawford children went to my daycare, Brandon being one of them. When my daughter had Mrs. Crawford for her 5th grade teacher, many years later, Brandon came to visit on career day (after winning the World Series) and how to follow their own dreams. When it was question time, my daughter Lexi raised her hand and said "my dad said that you and he used to throw the baseball in our backyard." Brandon said "that is true." Lexi raised her hand again and said "my dad says you are as good as you are because you and my dad threw the ball in our backyard." And Brandon said "that is not true." We both burst out laughing and from that moment on our meeting had risen to a higher level of intimacy. We now had something even more in common, a fantastic teacher that each of our children had experienced sometime in their academic lives and the teacher's local hero son.

As we descended the stairs to go back down she told me that she loved the home. It turns out that they were interested in downsizing, they owned a home in the same community that they thought would sell for $2.4 million, and that they wanted a home like our listing due to the location (on the golf course and her husband loves to play golf) and the backyard had a pool for her three children. Not only did we sell the home to them, but we were able to take our next luxury listing too. Sometimes good old fashioned talking is the best tool for connecting with clients!

Match Making: Our website is an important first impression

Our team manager spends many hours updating our website and keeping it informative and user friendly. Our website is often the first connection a new client makes with us as they search the web for homes that are listed with their specifications; we have met many luxury clients whose first connection with us was via our website. After they view listings on our site they either contact us using email or they pick up the phone and call us. We received a call from a potential buyer recently; he had viewed our team real estate website from Minnesota and was calling us to schedule viewing some luxury homes that we had listed on our site. What I loved about him from the start was his direct, informative approach. He spelled out that he wanted exactly; a 5000 to 6000-square foot home, a home to reflect his new position amongst other top executives, and a private yet a grand contemporary home for entertaining.

I have to be honest; we spend a lot of time updating our website. We were secretly thrilled that a potential buyer from across the country had located us due to our internet presence. All the strategizing, updating, and staying current actually pays off (thank you Kim!). To be a top producing agent amongst strong competition means we have to be competitive in every area. Building our website, especially geared around our luxury communities, is very important to us and it is definitely what caught this client's eye. He oozes the energy of power and luxury, He wears this image daily, it's just who he is and this vision came very clearly to me over the phone. In our first couple of minutes he said to me "I'm sure you have seen the news about me this morning" it was a statement not a question. I Googled him immediately when I got back to my office. I found out that he had just been appointed as a top fortune 500 executive in Pleasanton.

My belief is always being authentic in anything that you do; we try to live our lives this way. As luxury agents, we always try to find something with our client that we can relate to or that they can connect to us with. So we ask questions that will help us find this sincere connection. In this case I didn't stop to think when I asked him if his family would be coming to view the homes (based on the size of the home) or if he was solo on this first journey. He explained that he was divorced and that his dogs were too old to travel. I asked him "do you date?" he said "why are you going to sell me a home and ask me out?" I burst out laughing and said "No I have been married since I was 19, but I was thinking about my partner DeAnna." To this day I have no idea why I said that (without DeAnna's permission I might add) and it was definitely a risky thing to ask, not having anything to do with purchasing a house. But it was a lesson in trusting myself, plus it was fun to laugh together. Spoiler alert, they have never dated – but this story has been a great cocktail conversation!

He asked for two days to view a minimum of 15 homes. We set the dates and DeAnna and I selected 15 luxury homes that were currently on the market in Danville, San Ramon, and Pleasanton. One of his specifications was that he wanted a short commute to his company. We sent the previews and he chose the ones he wanted to view.

When he arrived we were excited to meet him in person! He was and is wonderful. His love for his work, his dogs and his cars came through. We made sure we had all our information in order, such as comparative marketing analysis (CMAs) for the areas that we had chosen to show him, water for the car, a timed lunch at one of the open homes that we knew were serving an old fashioned barbeque, our luxury roomy air conditioned car (since he wasn't used to sunny California), and our selected homes mapped out for minimum timing between homes so as not to waste his time. Our showings are very strategized to maximize our time together. Our motto is; always plan ahead and plan well and make sure we show our listed homes first and have our listed homes be the starting point. If at all possible we want to secure the buyer for one of our listings always keeping in mind the trust our seller has with us.

Our client right off loved Ruby Hill, from the executives living there, to the gated, golf course lifestyle. Ruby Hill characterizes luxury at its best. He picked out three homes that he liked; two were in Ruby Hill and one in Kottinger Ranch, another beautiful luxury subdivision in Pleasanton. The Kottinger home sits on top of a hill and has views all the way to Walnut Creek. It is absolutely stunning, definitely a home where you would feel "king of the castle" we showed this home to him because of its grandeur, size, location and the dramatic views. His commute would be cut by at least 20 minutes each way daily if he chose this home and we all know with luxury buyers that time is money.

He was great to work with because he wasn't emotionally attached to the potential home he was purchasing. He liked it, the flow of it, he could see himself living in it but if they didn't accept his offer he told us he would move onto his second choice. Even in a sellers' market, he came from a position of power that was pretty amazing. We have noticed this many times with luxury buyers. They choose first on the location, second on the flow of the home and third they are not attached to getting it if their "deal" isn't accepted. The strategy is very important to them; they enjoy being part of the offer and the negotiation process.

This listing agent for the Kottinger Ranch home was also a very well-respected agent in our area who we were excited to work with. In turn because of our reputation, she wanted to work with us. The extra plus came when I realized I knew the sellers, their son was in our high school car pool for many years. Keep in mind; it's always who you know and our client trusted us when we showed him this home even though he wasn't familiar with the area. The seller wanted to work with us because of our past relationship and the listing agent wanted to work with us because of our reputation for bringing in very qualified buyers.

After he moved into his new home, he told us one of the most endearing things about us as a team is our communication skills. He has referred us many times. We will always take calls, even with a time change. Even with a team manager and team assistant, we personally take calls, we email, we text. The bottom line is we stay connected with our clients. We keep the sale personal with our constant communication.

After working with him we found out that his new company has a relocation division. He chose to work with us instead of his company's relocation agent. And thanks to him, we got our foot in the door with his companies' relocation department. We currently are on their network of Realtors® serving the Bay Area.

Match Making Luxury Homes is not always Pretty!

DeAnna sold a notorious Castle Wood Golf Course

murder home, not once but twice! She worked with a luxury investor that loved the home from a financial aspect. He purchased it at a very low price because most people don't want to live in a home with this kind of stigma. This investor remodeled it and then relisted it with our team. He made a $200,000 profit in a short amount of time and we made the sale twice over because we aren't afraid to explore all phases of selling luxury real estate.

Match Making: Expect the Unexpected

I was hosting an open house in Ruby Hill on the golf course when a family with five sons came in. The parents wanted to see where the property line was in comparison with the golf course, so we all went outside to take a look. When we got back inside I noticed that there was a very large hawk sitting on the hearth. At first I thought it was stuffed but when it cawed loudly and raised it wings I knew it was very much alive. I calmly asked the family to take cover as I tried to shoo the grandfather hawk back outside. At the same time someone's cell phone went off I had been half way to the front door to open it. I heard a scream behind me and as I turned I saw the hawk flying straight for me (with a 4-5 foot wing span). I screamed and ran for the door, believing I would feel the talons on my back any minute. As luck would have it the hawk flew by me and landed on the couch in the living room. I calmly pried myself off the front door; turned back around and asked the family if they would be willing to sign into our iPad. I explained if they purchased this home they would always have a story to tell their children and friends for a lifetime. We always try to look and act professional even when something as unexpected as a hawk comes to visit (I'm not sure I succeed in this instance! HA!).

Match Making: Communication is "key" to Selling your Home

The foundation for quality in all relationships is communication. Communication between DeAnna and myself as a team is essential. We always answer each other's calls, text messages, and emails no matter where we are. On any given day we are available to each other. There is nothing more important to us than our clients. In a sense they are part of our family, their home is our home, and their questions are ours to answer. Communication with other agents, communication with lenders, and communication with our team is always at our forefront. In all phases of our real estate career with all the people that we come into contact with, highest on the list is communication.

We love to meet people, we like to learn about their lives, we like to touch their lives, we like to listen and we like to talk, we are the perfect blend of business, knowledge and fun. Even if it is just a passing greeting, meeting people excites us. Our luxury clients don't expect us to be like them, they don't need us to live in their neighborhood, they just want us to be familiar with where they live. They expect a high level of service where it is our honor to be a part of their real estate lives for a moment in time. Some clients like to text, some like to talk on the phone, some like to email, some like to Skype, some live in California, some live in different states, some live in different countries. We have versed ourselves in all phases of technology and communication so that we may be available to our clients easily on a daily time frame that works for them. Luxury clients want to know that we are available to them by the means that works best for them. Deanna recently had a client visiting from Virginia (they found us on the internet). She had to Skype with the client's husband back in Virginia because he could not travel due to work. They ended up purchasing a $2.5 million home, even though the husband had never set foot in the home.

Success for our luxury sellers is equal to our success for our luxury buyers. We can't have one without the other. We use technology of all forms so our transactions are a win, win for everyone. Recently we had a Zillow lead pop up on my phone that said: "Make me want to sell." The home address was in Ruby Hill. I contacted the homeowner and she said that "her husband had put that on the internet without her knowledge" she said that "I was the 4th person to call." I talked to her about getting our client in to see their home; it was just what our clients had been looking for. She wanted all the agents to come on Saturday. I asked if we could come right away and she agreed. In short, DeAnna ended up representing the seller, I represented the buyers and we put the deal together for both sides that day before any other agents had a chance to view the home. To top it off, DeAnna was on vacation and I was in the office. She and I had to really work all phases of technology such as: cell phones, Docu-sign, emails, text messaging, internet sites, and Skyping – we were successful in getting the sellers the most for their home and the buyers got the home of their dreams. This was the perfect Match.

ABOUT THE AUTHORS:
Liz Venema
DeAnna Armario

Match Making: The Value of Hiring a Top Producing Team

DeAnna Armario and Liz Venema, of Armario Venema Homes, are a top producing real estate team based in Pleasanton, California. Last year, they generated $30 million in home sales. This year, they are on target to double that. They are the difference between Ordinary and Extraordinary!

"Our thrill is finding the perfect match for your home. We are matchmakers, we listen to what you love about your home, we note the specifics, and then we go about finding that perfect buyer just for you. Our plan is tri-fold: Positioning, Marketing, and Negotiation.

We are equal partners. What this means to our luxury clients is basically that you get two top professional Realtors® for the price of one. Our success as a team, our great partnership, and how well we work together for our clients is always our number one selling point. We are committed to getting our clients top dollar for their home.

We each have our strengths. DeAnna is the closer in many transactions. She is more analytical and works really well with numbers. I tend to be the lead generator-I love the heart connection of real estate. I learned early on that people just want to be heard and we take the time to hear them. We learn about their desires and then find ways that we can help them achieve their dreams in real estate. We both put our clients first at all times. This mantra is the foundation of our business. We have built our amazing partnership on working smart, maximizing our time, and choosing wisely what we want to focus our attention on. We have risen to a higher level of real estate mainly due to the fact that we are like-minded in our approach for our clients. They appreciate our energy and enthusiasm, coupled with our detail-oriented approach. Our talents for listening to our clients, taking action on their behalf, and believing in them are the qualities that make us successful.

From the moment we started to work together, we just clicked. DeAnna has more real estate experience than I do, but I have many local contacts. I grew up in luxury homes. My dad was a builder and a developer. I watched him from an early age build homes and listen to his clients. What they wanted above all else was quality. That is what DeAnna and I try to bring to all our clients today: quality in our communication, quality in our marketing, and quality in our personal presence.

Having raised our families in the East Bay area, DeAnna and I appreciate the diversity of this area and have first-hand knowledge of our top rated schools, sports leagues, and community events. We work in the community where we live and this is a priceless asset to our clients, whether they are relocating from the East coast or from the other side of town.

From comprehensive listing preparation, expert negotiation skills, strategic marketing, and in depth market knowledge, we will make your transaction a pleasurable, positive experience whether you are selling, buying-or both."

~Liz and DeAnna
You can find Liz and DeAnna at www.ArmarioVenemaHomes. com; email Liz@VenemaHomes.com or DeAnna@Armario-Homes.com; or call, Liz 925.413.6544 and DeAnna 925.260.2220.

Chapter 9

Every Home
Tells a Story

By Sandi Solomonson

Reno and Incline Village, Nevada

Every home tells a story, and bringing forth all that a home has to offer with creative and exceptional strategies translates to exceptional results for the people I serve. During the entire listing and escrow process, my clients know I have thick skin and broad shoulders, which re-assures them of my resolve to bring about creative solutions for any challenges that may pop up.

For me, home is Reno, Nevada. Relocating here from the beautiful Sonoma Wine Country in the San Francisco Bay Area, I was drawn to the wide open spaces, Nevada's friendly tax environment, and the quality and quantity of life. In fact, on average, we enjoy 310 days of clear blue skies and sunshine each year. So, even if it gets chilly, you find yourself still reaching for those sunglasses. This entire region is known for a plethora of events, ease of travel, great restaurants, entertainment, and an emphasis on locally grown food.

I chose this area for its natural beauty, snowcapped mountains, and expansive valleys. With Reno being a bike-friendly city, and my property backing up to protected wetlands, it's easy to bike to the movies, or the farmers market. Of course, waking up to stunning views and relaxing with gorgeous sunsets helps too.

When not working in Reno, you'll find me helping clients in Incline Village, on the west shores of Lake Tahoe. Known for being a tax haven plus its wealthy, notable residents, this small community includes private beaches, recreational privileges, rich history, and the crowning glory, the second deepest lake in the USA. No wonder visitors come from around the world to Lake Tahoe, and why buyers seek to own property in this resort community.

Practicing a Philosophy of Gratitude

I like to bring gratitude into everything of life; including every aspect of my business. I'm a firm believer that nothing is random and feel an appreciation for every luxury seller and buyer I have the opportunity to work with. Additionally, I delight in demonstrating an extra measure of care with clients; the little things such as bringing snacks and beverages to inspections, picking up lunch for the photographer, and coming to the table fully prepared to negotiate on behalf of my client's interests. One time, I even found myself on the floor, keeping a toddler occupied so the parents could casually walk through a property at their leisure. Since starting my business in 2006 at Lake Tahoe, it's been a pleasure to expand into the Reno region; incorporating luxury sellers and cross-marketing with an emphasis on Nevada tax advantages and resort living.

Marketing with Enthusiasm, Quality and Zest

In one instance, I had the opportunity to help a client sell her home after it had been on the market for more than two years. Being her third Realtor®, she was understandably frustrated and sad that her goal of retiring with the proceeds from the sale of this property had not come to fruition. Once we met, I knew the home could sell and the pricing wasn't far off. The listing price we finalized of more than $1 million made the seller happy. It was critical to identify the audience for this property, which was a ranchette with stunning valley views. An added bonus was a large industrial shop that included a guest apartment. I began to think about who might appreciate this unique home. The profiles that I pictured as probable were buyers such as artists, collectors, musicians wanting a recording studio, families with live-in parents, people who work from home; or people who like to entertain guests. The marketing plan included a draw for out- of-state buyers seeking Nevada tax advantages, professionals who may work from home, and individuals seeking shop space to pursue hobbies or projects. Building the right message to reach the right buyer was a significant part of marketing this property. Within 90 days we sold the home! The seller was able to retire and start a new chapter in life; needless to say, she was tickled pink!

It's important to note the pricing structure didn't change from previous listing agents. By directing better photography, creating a more comprehensive marketing portfolio, and pumping up the level of marketing to better appeal to luxury buyers, the message easily connected with the right buyer. The home was able to attract a better caliber of buyers from a larger geographic area. It worked! The buyer and seller both achieved their goals.

Creative Solutions to Sticky Problems

When creative solutions emerge to solve sticky problems, I always extend gratitude to all involved. I look for solutions, and then when solutions become clear, I like to send thank you notes to everyone involved for resolving whatever situations may emerge in a real estate transaction.

In one instance, I was working with the seller on a home for sale in Incline Village. We were able to obtain an offer pretty easily from a pre-qualified buyer. This was a beautiful home, but the seller was going to be losing money. He had bought the house somewhat recently, and had put money into it for nice renovations. Based on the current market value, he was going to be losing money on the sale, and would have to bring in cash to close escrow.

The buyer liked the home but as we went into escrow, we ended up getting into a sticky situation that could have ended the transaction. Because the home was so unique, and the banks had increased restrictions on homes they would approve for lending, the buyer's lender declined to fund the loan. We were in a situation that required creative diligence to come up with a solution. I was thinking about the situation and suggested the seller provide seller-financing on the home to the buyer. This worked out smoothly for both seller and buyer. Plus, because the seller would be earning interest on the loan, he could make back some of the loss that he had incurred.

When a creative solution solves an escrow situation, it becomes a win-win for all involved. Without the seller financing, the buyer would not have gotten the home they wanted. And the seller would have been in a weakened position knowing that some banks may decline to lend on his property in the changed bank environment. The solution worked out for everyone.

When the Seller Won't Let Go

In this scenario, the sellers had a very strong emotional attachment to the home they had owned for a long time. I was representing the buyer, and when we offered the first time, the offer was rejected. I began to think through the situation, because my buyers very much wanted to own this home. I sensed the strong emotional ties that the seller had with the home and decided to meet emotion with emotion.

As I went over the situation with the buyer, we came up with a plan. They increased the offer a small amount – not the price the sellers were asking that was far over the market value – but a small amount so that I could bring the offer freshly in front of the seller. We built a very warm and friendly package showing the photographs of the buyers, and even included the names of their children. We talked about how the new buyers would love and care for the home – just as the sellers had for so many years. This was successful! The home went into escrow and buyer and seller were happy with the result.

The Principal of Sacrifice

This was a home for sale in Incline Village, and it did not have a garage. Beyond that, you could not easily get to the home! You had to climb down stairs so access to the condominium was a challenge. The home was not updated, and basically every room needed to be remodeled. My clients were seeking $2 million for the home, so I felt I had my work cut out for me.

We wanted to create a story that would hit the specific buyer who could buy and enjoy this home. It would not have been a good idea to gloss over the lack of garage or outdated interior. The home had one thing going for it – toes in the sand from the front door in moments – and a sweeping inspirational view of the lake that could make waking up joyful however many days a year the buyer wishes to occupy the home.

So the principal of sacrifice means that you do not hide the negative component of the home. We put that right out in front of everyone. I included language about the home that showed it to be close to the freeway, without a garage, and with a slight challenge to access. On the bright side, the panoramic view of Lake Tahoe was spellbinding.

The home sold for very close to the asking price, with a $1,850,000 sold price on a $1,998,000 list price. I marketed the property to the buyer who would love the location. Someone bought the home from another state, who wanted to come a few times each year and unplug. The buyer did not care about the outdated interior or the fact you had to walk down a few steps to get to the property.

The beauty of this solution was that we just shone light very brightly on all of the positive components of the condominium but also shone light on the rather glaring aspects that buyers typically dislike. We were very up front and the home sold very fast for a great price.

Every Home Tells a Story

I work hard to provide an emotional connection to a home for the potential buyer. When you create emotion over the internet-for instance with historical detail that garners attention, possibly giving the property a formal title, or communicate the lifestyle of the area, then you can reach out to new audiences with the home's personalized message.

Part of this process includes researching a luxury home with great depth. I look for stories about the builder; a notable figure that owned or visited the property, or any part the home has played in local history. Some homes also offer amazing custom features that may include the unique or eccentric which buyers love to read about. This research opens the door to reach out to select groups of people who might become buyers. I work carefully with a photographer that shares my conviction of quality in still shots and well-crafted virtual tours which serves well to communicate the story or emotional connection of a home over an otherwise sterile internet. This may include hiking out into a marsh or up a steep hill to get the perfect shot. I like to put life and energy into the marketing.

It takes intention and creativity to connect with a buyer who may be living in other parts of the world. I like to share property details, both the positive and the draw-backs; you won't ever see the basic "three-bedroom, two bath" description on any home I am selling. Buyers have a short attention span, so relaying information in a concise, engaging manner works to make that connection.

Besides property details, I enjoy bringing the lifestyle into the marketing. Painting a picture of the Lake Tahoe and Reno lifestyle and culture that I truly believe in myself works to accentuate my listings and offers the buyer a snapshot of what life will be like in their new home. Even recognizing that some luxury buyers are seeking more "quantity" of life; something this region offers with less commuting, more time with their families and loved ones; plus, outdoor activities available in this year-round sports mecca can benefit a seller's marketing plan. Time is a precious commodity.

The Satisfaction of a Job Well Done

Nothing gives me more joy than seeing the right buyer land the home that I marketed for the seller, or seeing the buyers I represented find the exact luxury home that fits their lifestyle and vision for themselves. When I'm in Incline Village now, I will know families who come at the same time each year and enjoy all that Incline Village has to offer because I was able to get them into the right property that became a great fit.

In Reno, I find that the new homeowners I have matched with homes here are able to enjoy a lifestyle with more time, less traffic, less stress, great tax advantages, and more open space. The appreciation I have for this community grows as the city here grows. I know what it is like to live in the more densely populated areas of Northern California, and I am content that I have made my home in the state of Nevada.

The feedback that matters the most to me is the feedback and referrals of clients I have served. I build my business by referrals and this is the testimony that gives me fuel. It is this feeling of satisfaction from my clients that drives me to continue to do my best, learn more, serve with more zest, and solve any tricky problems that arise with as much creativity and intelligence I can bring to the table. As always, I stand in gratitude for every challenge that awaits. Life is always full of surprises.

ABOUT THE AUTHOR: *Sandi Solomonson*

Since starting her career, Sandi Solomonson has demonstrated extraordinary success as a Realtor® in the Reno and Incline Village region of Nevada. She is recognized for bringing unparalleled strengths to her clients including residential real estate and more recently, creating a full team to relocate companies and individuals to Nevada for Tax Advantages. "It's always exciting to see clients light up when they realize how Nevada Tax Advantages can benefit their individual portfolios and corporate profitability. My clients are often amazed at the increase of quality and quantity of life here in Northern Nevada."

Her in-depth knowledge of the region and marketing savvy are keys to her success in the luxury home market. With tenacity, discretion, and integrity, she goes the extra mile to bring about a successful transaction for buyers and sellers alike. "My greatest motivation is to ensure my clients financial goals and real estate interests."

A native Californian, Sandi calls Northern Nevada home. When enjoying down time, you will find her out hiking, snowshoeing, singing jazz, creating music, and entertaining. In fact, more often than not, many clients become valued friends.

With offices in Incline Village, Lake Tahoe and Reno, Sandi looks forward to using her steadfast approach to benefit her clients.

Contact Sandi Solomonson at www.SandiSolomonson.com.

Chapter 10

Welcome to Seattle

By Joseph Ho

Seattle, Washington

Seattle, commonly known as the Emerald City, is ideally located on the West Coast between Vancouver B.C. and San Francisco. Seattle is flanked by the Cascade Mountains to the east; the Olympic Mountains and Puget Sound to the west; with the shores of Lake Washington tucked between Seattle and the neighboring city of Bellevue. The two cities are serviced by two floating bridges, 520 and I-90. There is also Lake Sammamish to the east of Bellevue. There are so many Luxury Home choices from view homes to waterfront to secluded acre plus estates all within city limits.

This hidden gem has recently been discovered by

others, most notably by foreign nationals and many from China looking for the lifestyle and beautiful environment that few cities can rival. With 30 years of experience in the Greater Seattle real estate market, I've noted a recent trend has emerged. This chapter will highlight some first-hand experiences and best practices on how to best service clients from around the globe in purchasing luxury homes in our area.

The first rule of real estate is LOCATION, LOCATION, LOCATION. Right behind that is VALUE, which is dictated by supply and demand. Demand is the game-changer and with the recent interest from foreign nationals, it has driven the upward trend in values for our area.

For a number of years, Seattle was skipped over by the international investor. They would visit Vancouver BC, fly over Seattle, and choose San Francisco or Los Angeles. These cities were in demand because of the amenities and cultural comforts they provided: language, food, restaurants, etc. However, in the past three years, Seattle hit the map as a destination to consider. In 2013 there was a very popular Chinese movie titled "Finding Mr. Right" also known as "Beijing Meets Seattle," featuring Seattle as the setting. This film brought fantastic exposure for Seattle.

Once newcomers discover Seattle, the first remarks are usually "It is so green and the air is so clean" and

"The lakes and mountains are beautiful." The typical itinerary will be a five- to seven-day visit in the Greater Seattle area followed by a drive up to Vancouver, British Columbia for a day trip. Then many will go on to San Francisco and Los Angeles, sometimes with a detour to Las Vegas. The most desirable luxury homes are waterfront, then view and acreage estates. Waterfront homes are at the top of this list with Lake Washington in particular. This lake is unique for the yachting lifestyle as the only fresh water lake that allows access to the Puget Sound and Pacific Ocean. This is accomplished by navigating from the lake to the Ballard locks then into the Puget Sound. This is unique to Seattle and not available in Vancouver, San Francisco or Los Angeles.

What these buyers are looking for is the lifestyle a luxury home and neighborhood provides. The lifestyle for their children is also a consideration. For many years, international buyers would come to our area because their child was going to attend college. A recent trend has been that they bring children for the high school education as well. In this way, families may adapt and acclimate to America and the language rather than a lone child starting in a new country and language for the first time when in college. This has raised the importance of neighborhoods with good high schools. The following public high schools are rated in the top 100 in the US: International, Bellevue, Newport, Interlake and Mercer Island.

I work hard to assist foreign clients with the home buying process in America, much like a first time homebuyer. For the international buyer, there are additional steps and it is also important to understand cultural differences and preferences.

Understanding Feng Shui

Feng Shui is an ancient principle of Chinese culture. It is essentially a home's balance with nature and primarily with how a house is designed and oriented. I will touch on just some of the basic principles:

• Prefer that the front door faces south or southeast.

• Dislike staircase that faces directly to the front door.

• Dislike the front door facing the back door.

• Dislike doors that face another door directly across in hallways.

• Dislike kitchens beneath the master bedroom, especially the stove.

• Dislike house or street numbers that end in the number four.

• Really like the number eight, the more the better.

Although these are important, each valued independently is not necessarily a deal-breaker. Once, I was able to get the house number changed from a four to an eight which made for a very happy client. For some buyers Feng Shui is so important that they may want to make an offer subject to a Feng Shui Master checking out the house, much like a structural inspection.

Financing and Closing Process for the International Buyer

Although some international buyers can pay all cash, it can be beneficial to get a loan when interest rates are low. There are only a handful of banks that can do these types of loans. Many of these buyers have no social security numbers, no credit history, and assets may be difficult to document. With that said, there are banks that will do these loans usually because they have branches in their native countries. Check around your local communities to see if such a bank exists. The loan to value is usually 60 percent. Another factor is getting funds into the United States, countries like China and Korea may only allow $50,000 per person per year.

Refer international clients to a savvy bank or financial expert to best help them. This is another specialist to have on your team. Be very careful when an international buyer wishes to pay all cash, as it is important to make sure the cash is in U.S. dollars already and they can provide proof of funds on deposit.

Making offers is always fun. Many times the foreign buyer will want to make low offers, as that is a part of their culture. Some education is needed for both buyers and sellers. I try to encourage reasonable offers by showing as many comparables as possible. If a foreign buyer still insists on making a very low offer, I will make the offer for them and prepare them for a counter. I explain that I will do my very best to get the offer accepted, but I also get a commitment from them to ensure that if I get a good counter offer they will proceed with the transaction. I will usually ask to present the offer personally with the listing agent. The first thing I explain to the Seller is that they should not take the low offer personally, and I explain that the buyers really do like their house. The initial low offer is just the way they are accustomed to doing business. Many sellers of luxury homes are well traveled and very understanding. I have never been thrown out of a house no matter how low the offer. I made an offer of $15 million on a $26 million house once and the seller would not counter for five days. The buyer flew to Malibu on the sixth day and made an offer on an ocean front home instead. Buyers have choices, they can pick from anywhere along the west coast. The lesson learned is to counter and counter again, it's what I call the "deal dance". You can't find a partner if you don't dance.

Inspection is also important just like any normal transaction. If there is a good experienced licensed inspector who is bilingual in the language of the foreign buyer, it makes things a little easier. If not, it's not a big deal as the reports are usually written with pictures that you review in detail with them.

Title and escrow may be a whole new concept. I am fortunate to work with a title and escrow company that has escrow officers who speak multiple languages. I always accompany all my clients to escrow regardless of language. Another professional you may want to add to your team is a good tax attorney who can advise them on the best entity to take title of the property depending on state and federal tax laws. Some of my clients will take title under an LLC or trust for tax and estate reasons.

I like to work carefully with my clients to understand their plans for the house.

Do they like the property "as is"? Are they thinking of remodeling?

Once, I sold a multi-million dollar house and his plans were to demolish it and build new on a beautiful piece of waterfront property. My client was a very successful real estate developer in China. During the feasibility period, I made sure I found a Mandarin-speaking architect to look at the house with this client. Then I took them out to lunch and made sure the architect explained to him step-by-step what our building process and timeline would be like. In our area it would be a two to three-year process from start to finish if lucky and without unexpected delays. During this conversation I could see the look of amazement in his eyes as the conversation went on. At the end, I asked what he had thought the building process would be like. He looked at me and said "I thought it would take three months." In China, one floor of a high rise can be built in a week. It is very important to educate clients from other countries on the process and managing expectations. He still bought the house because it was a great property.

Lifestyle and After the Close of Escrow Service

After the purchase agreement is signed, and depending on their budget. I may take my clients to the Rolls Royce or Mercedes dealership and then the yacht dealer. Sometimes I'll drop them off at the furniture store, the high end luxury shopping center, and even the casino. This shows them the lifestyle their new home will provide them. I once took a client to the Rolls Royce dealership and he looked at a brand new Phantom for $500,000 dollars. He said to me "I have this exact car in China that I paid a million dollars for. Here I can buy two." There are very high taxes on luxury items in China. At the furniture store, I worked out a deal with the owner to give my clients a 35 percent discount. I or my assistant will pick them up and drop them off at the airport. When I drop them off at the airport, I give them a quarter to keep with their passport. I tell them to call me after they clear customs on their next visit. It leaves a great impression when I or my assistant is the first and last smiling face they see.

After closing, if my clients don't have friends or relatives in the area, I will offer to take care of the property for them. My assistant will check the mail, and pay the utilities, gardening, and other maintenance bills. They will leave me a few thousand dollars or more depending on the size of the property and we send them a quarterly expense and balance report. I've had clients that don't return for up to a year. I really focus on working the relationships and not just the transaction.

ABOUT THE AUTHOR: *JOSEPH HO*

Over the last three decades, Joseph Ho has become one of the most trusted and acclaimed real estate brokers in the Greater Seattle Area. Known and acknowledged amongst public and peers for his integrity, experience, knowledge and award winning service, he has won numerous service and marketing awards including the Seattle Distinguished Sales and Marketing Award for all marketing industries, the MAME Grand Award for New Construction Marketing and the Legend Award for Prudential Real Estate for consecutive years as a Top 1 percent Broker nationally. Joseph has been interviewed by world-wide media including Bloomberg News, CCTV, MSNBC, Seattle Times and quoted in numerous news and radio articles. He is regarded as one of the very rare real estate brokers with the ability and expertise to complete both residential and complex commercial transactions. His expertise has evolved over the years as his clients trusted only Joseph to help them with all things real estate. His clients range from the grandson of a favorite client buying his first $50,000 condo to the sale of a $33 million Downtown Bellevue apartment complex to Equity Residential, a Fortune 500 Corporation. Joseph attributes his success to working on the best interests of his clients and life long relationships, not just a one-time sale or transaction. The greatest reward for Joseph has been the many clients who have become great life long friends.

You can find Joseph at www.JosephHo.net.

Chapter 11

The Heart
of the Matter

By Kate Carcone

Ontario, Canada

Passion rules in real estate. It's a 24-7 business and you have to love it to really succeed. It takes heart.

The first signs of my budding passion for the business started early. In my early teens, I would spend hours reading Architectural Digest and leafing through every home decorating magazine and book I could get my hands on. I have always been fascinated by houses and I have an absolute love and respect for beautiful homes.

When a house is filled with people, it hums with

energy and life. That human life-force is the essential difference between a house and home. Every house is unique, every structure tells a story. My task as a Luxury Home Marketing Specialist is to tell that story, and to package and showcase each property to its maximum advantage.

Truth be told, I always knew I wanted to be a Real Estate Broker. In high school, I was asked to interview a professional in the industry I wished to aspire to. When I told my teacher I wanted to be a Real Estate Broker she told me it was nice to have dreams but that I was most likely to become an accountant. Ever the eternal optimist – I sat down with a local agent and interviewed her in the kitchen of her stunning Willow Tree Farm Estate Home. Today, we are close friends and work out of the same office. She gave me the most valuable piece of advice – find a mentor and follow their every move.

Finding a Mentor

I am enormously fortunate and grateful that my mother, Marion Carcone, is my mentor. A 25-year veteran in the industry, my mother is at the top of our local market rankings and is among the top 100 Realtors® in Canada. She is a trailblazer known for being smart, tenacious, savvy, and incredibly creative. Although she is highly sought after by her clients and has received numerous industry accolades, it is her humble nature and complete lack of ego that really shine through. I admit, I may be biased, but I truly admire her business style and I fashion my own approach closely after hers.

We currently work out of the same office, and although we each run our own separate book of business, she has taught me everything I know about real estate sales and service. She never handed over business – but she did teach me how to get business, and how to manage a transaction. Not everyone will be so blessed to have a loved one be their professional mentor, but I am always amazed by the generosity of talented people who are willing to share their insights and experiences with others.

Marketing a Luxury Home

I am often asked the question "how do you market a luxury home?" In short: it takes passion, patience, strategy, and a tailor-made marketing plan. As with any house, each luxury home has its own collection of challenges.

My role as a Luxury Home Marketing Specialist is to make the houses I represent beautiful. It is to market and communicate a home's unique and most attractive features and tell the story of the home through the eyes of a potential buyer. My marketing programs are based on the themes of Style and Sophistication, Luxury and Beauty.

In the words of the Great Zig Ziglar, "People don't buy for logical reasons, they buy for emotional reasons". Any real estate professional would whole-heartedly agree. I have worked with clients from a wide range of industry backgrounds – many of whom operate in rigorous, fact- based professions. Most want all the critical 'bricks and mortar' statistics: number of bedrooms, square footage, recent sales on the street and the list goes on. In almost all cases, however, I have found that people buy with the heart – real estate has an enormous emotional aspect that is integral to the entire transaction.

Understanding what moves a buyer is the key to presenting a house that will fit their needs and desires.

My Process

As a Luxury Home Marketing Specialist, my first visit to any property always involves a detailed viewing of the house – inside and out. I carry a notebook and make detailed notes on every aspect of the structure. When permitted, I take photos that I will use to jog my memory when needed and to highlight and reference when establishing value. When I receive a call asking about a particular room or feature – I can immediately reference the photo and handle any objections with authority. After the site visit, I regroup over my notes and photos making a detailed list of the subject property plusses and objectionables.

When negotiating a contract, no buyer will provide the list of great property features; they will however provide you a list of all the negatives. My job is to mitigate objections before they appear. I carefully examine the list of objectionables and immediately go to work on how to either repair or repurpose each line item. In some rare cases we repurpose entire rooms, or provide remodeling where needed.

Setting the Stage

I cannot emphasize enough the power of staging and repurposing rooms. Selling houses is about telling a story – a story about the home and what the life within its walls will deliver. Some buyers are looking for a quiet solstice away from work, some are looking for a luxe, high glamour entertaining pad, while others still are looking for a functional place to raise or start a family. My role is to understand what a buyer is looking for – what motivates them - and deliver that dream on a platter.

Delivering the Dream: Staging and Other Tips

I remember showing a property to Sara and John, a couple who had lived overseas for 12 years. When viewing the property, Sara remarked how wonderful the house would look at Christmas; it had a beautiful stone fireplace, a grand entry with white picket stairs and an over-sized dining room. Sara remarked how much she loved the house and how it would be the perfect house to host her extended family over the holidays. Prior to their second visit I asked my home stagger to pull together every piece of Christmas décor she could – a challenging task given that it was July.

We managed to decorate the house for the perfect family Christmas. We used garland, put up a tree, and even set a Christmas table in the dining room – service for 16. The house looked beautiful - like a perfect holiday window at Macy's on 34th.

When Sara and John returned – they were thrilled! We delivered their dream and they purchased the home the next day.

Staging is just that - setting a stage and telling a story. To tell the story well you need to understand the buyer and their needs and tailor your staging to achieve a happy ending. Staging really is about delivering the dream.

Marketing Pieces

I'm often asked "What marketing pieces should you prepare for a luxury property?". In short, spare no expense. I am always amazed that some Realtors® skimp on take-away marketing pieces. It is a grave injustice to the homes they represent. My recommendation is to find the best photographer in your area

– and use them. A great photographer is worth their weight in gold. Most buyers visit a property twice before making a purchasing decision. In almost all cases, the buyer will make a decision while sitting in their current residence leafing through your feature sheets or virtual tour. Always, always, always spend money here!

Your property feature sheet should be full of color with plenty of photos, less copy, and be professionally printed and formatted. It should be a statement of style with your particular brand coupled with the properties unique features carefully captured and communicated. I suggest finding a graphic designer to put together a standard feature sheet that aligns with your marketing message and local market. I spent two months last summer with a graphic designer – redesigning my property marketing take-aways and feature sheets. To date, during broker open houses I am always asked by other brokers for a copy of my feature sheets. My designer certainly did a terrific job of designing a marketing piece that communicates style, sophistication, and beauty.

The Importance of a Floor Plan

For every new listing, I prepare a floor plan with room measurements. I keep the floor plan on file, alongside a floor plan with the current room names omitted. My reason for this is simple; most buyers will not remember an entire house floor plan by memory. They will however walk through a property for the first time and repurpose rooms to fit their own needs – libraries will become art studios, game rooms will become media rooms and so on. When I send a floor plan over to the potential buyer or buyer agent, I rename each room according to the buyers needs. It helps the buyer reaffirm their memory of the property and helps in packaging the house for the 'right fit'.

Going to Market

Once the property has been staged and positioned for profit, and the marketing pieces prepared, the next step is the introduction to market. The internet is the number one medium for positioning real estate. Do not overlook the value of your networking groups and local Realtor® colleagues. I always host a broker open house event for a new listing. I serve lunch and send out invitations to the local brokers I want to attend. There is a great probability that among the brokers who do attend – that one will have a buyer that is the right fit for the property. I place enormous importance on continuing to develop a collaborative network of real estate brokers and industry professionals. More than half of all my listing sales come from my network; I have a tremendous respect for my colleagues in the business.

The Final Factor: Superior Customer Service

The theme of my marketing plans and materials is always centered around style and sophistication, but the engine that drives my business is always delivering superior customer service.

My commitment to excellence in my sales service is at the core of everything that I do. I feel fortunate to represent some of the most fascinating and influential individuals in my market. They are smart and know exactly what they want. They think big, dream big, and have huge expectations.

Excellent service means going above and beyond what is expected. It is about being completely passionate about what you do. The luxury house marketing sets the bar high and challenges us to be ultra creative, break boundaries, and find new channels to communicate our messages. I am a huge proponent of industry seminars and education. I regularly attend seminars to keep competitive and collaborate with my colleagues.

If I had to summarize what it takes to be an excellent luxury home broker I would say it in less than three words – it takes heart.

ABOUT THE AUTHOR: *KATE CARCONE*

Kate Carcone is a full-service real estate broker providing boutique style real estate council and sales service. She works under the Re/Max banner, employed under the umbrella of one of Toronto's largest Real Estate Offices – Re/Max Hallmark York Group Ltd.

Kate made her early start in real estate by trading investment property. To date she services an active client list of investors from Europe, Asia and the Middle East.

As a real estate broker, Kate maintains a license to trade commercial and residential real estate. She works more actively servicing clients in the residential market.

Kate's outstanding commitment to her clients awarded her a number of industry accolades including: 100 Club, Platinum Club, and induction to the Re/Max Hall of Fame. She is a dedicated industry professional consistently earning a top ten ranking within the Re/Max Hallmark York Group Realty standings.

Kate went on further in her real estate career to attain her CLHMS designation. A production based industry acknowledgement granted to proven professionals within the luxury home market niche. Certified as a Luxury Home Market Specialist (CLHMS) by the Institute for Luxury Home Marketing (ILHMS);

Kate has been honoured to represent some of the finest luxury properties in the GTA. From panoramic penthouses to private estates – Kate has excelled in standing behind and successfully marketing these unique properties.

In June 2013, Kate was inducted into the Million Dollar Guild (ILHMS) for her outstanding marketing and Sales Achievements within the luxury arena.

Kate regularly attends ILHMS "by invitation only" member meetings and conferences to discuss trends in the luxury market, and to maintain a competitive edge on behalf of her clients. As a designee and active ILHMS alumni member Kate has access to the very best tools and networks in the business. Kate is a true professional who is passionate about her work and committed to excellence in all she does.

You can find Kate at www.EstateKate.com.

Chapter 12

The Here and Now

By Nick Sylvester

Charlotte, North Carolina

The city of Charlotte, North Carolina is a very exciting place to be in the world of Luxury Real Estate. The metropolitan area has approximately 2.5 million people and growing very rapidly. A luxury property in this area could be anywhere from about $750,000 to about $5 million and a bit more. This part of the country is still mostly dominated by the small, local boutique firms that have catered to the luxury properties for many years. These firms are very good and quite well versed in the local area but the dynamic of the city is changing. Luxury property transactions are more and more often taking place on a national or even international level over great distances. This is where my expertise comes into play, my use of video production and media transmission as a marketing method for luxury property. I want to answer the question , how do I get the best and most accurate depiction of this property captured, and then packaged in a way that it can be shown to the most people who are likely to want to purchase it. The property must be shown in a very favorable light, and the desired viewer need be actively looking to purchase and be able to do so.

An example of this would be a client that I am working on a listing strategy and video presentation for. He owns two similar properties in the same affluent neighborhood in Charlotte, both are about 10,000+ square feet and will have a price point of just under $2 million each. These properties are both vacant and have been marketed in the past for a couple years without success. With knowledge of the market here we must come to terms that on a local level, the number of buyers willing and able to purchase one or both of these homes is few. I am not even considering starting traditional listings for this client because I know that a national or international campaign would greatly increase the odds of selling the properties. Homes like these, especially if vacant, must be brought to life, the lifestyle here must be created through sight, sound and motion....by video. The simple yet popular act of staging and nice aerial view pictures will more than likely not be enough in situations like this. This particular project is still in the works, due to the larger upfront costs, the owner needs to be involved so those negotiations are still ongoing. More about this story later.

The Passion

Luxury Real Estate and the act of brokering a deal either on the buyer or seller end is not the same as the traditional lower price point activity. Although the mechanics are the same, I feel that luxury is a lifestyle or a passion that one either embraces or does not. The luxury client is known for demanding only the best in service, performance, exclusivity confidentiality and attention to detail….the very things this client and the luxury agent demand from themselves. This, in my opinion, is the most important factor to being a successful agent at the luxury level.

Living a few miles south of L.A. for 15 years does take its toll on a person but it also will bestow its many virtues on you as well if open to it. L.A. is similar to New York in the saying "if you make it there, you make it anywhere". It is bold, intense, competitive and sometimes brash and unforgiving. This environment has taught me confidence, and the desire to always look for a better way to do the job. I imagine that I was there long enough for the film, music and entertainment world rubbed off on me. This is where the ideas of mixing video and Luxury Real Estate marketing/ listing/lead generation/ became one of my works in progress. This was way back before the latest wave of real estate reality show were on the air, now it is almost like a real estate frenzy when you turn on the set. There are so many DIY shows, or flip that house shows, interior design, million dollar this or that, it truly seems that we are ready for a change from traditional real estate marketing to its video alternative.

The more time I spend with long time Charlotte agents, the more I am told that I just don't think like an agent. With my background, I am able to use tools and strategies that are by no means traditional and certainly not conservative. I have the desire to create something that will give the property the best chance to sell right now. I still struggle with the 'list, wait and hope" methods. When I talk about using video I don't mean the virtual tour slide show with the elevator music. With the video and editing technology available today, we are making high quality, digital productions that showcase the property in a way that is quite unique and appealing. A video can reveal the house, the neighborhood, the amenities and certain attractions that are near by the property that is being listed for sale. Now don't get me wrong, this is a project that is still being tweaked and adjusted as we go forward with it. I have found myself in between video crews more than once for sure. There can be licensing issues, difference in opinions and many other creative issues that are not easy to solve. This also can be an expensive and complex way of marketing but I feel it is a long overdue way of the future of real estate, especially in the Luxury Market.

The Process

Years ago, I had some experiences with the film and TV industry and learned a lot about the creation of movies and shows as well as what it takes to get professional content.

With that said, I want to be clear that I do not pretend to be able to get behind a $10,000+ video camera and film a scene or handle sound and lights. To be successful at this, true technicians that have been to school for camera, lights, sound and editing must be used. The trick is done behind the scenes by the editor, that job should be left to the professionals, I won't even try to get involved with that. So depending on the budget and the size of the job, I will have one or two videographers, a sound man, a lights man and an editor. Now one guy could be the camera and editor or double up on sound and lights or something of that nature, but you can get away with using a couple skilled people and yourself helping direct the bit with no problem.

The goal of all of this is basically a three-pronged attack. The video can be used for at least three different tasks in the luxury listing and selling process. The first thing the video can serve as is a powerful demonstration tool used to market the agent and his team, showing a prior or demo video of this quality can be a great thing to bring to a big listing appointment presentation. Second, once the listing is obtained, the agent and video crew have the opportunity to breathe life into the property in a way that pictures just cannot. This is where skill and creativity come in as well as the style of the team doing the creating.

Depending on the desired outcome of a specific video, I might bring in a specific individual to be on screen touring the property and area, or I may do it myself for a different flavor. What I try to do is imagine someone out of town viewing the video that knows nothing about the property location, but is considering Charlotte as a home. What shots, features, angles or special amenities would persuade him to come schedule a showing in person. It has been proven many times that different people react differently to different kinds of stimulus, mainly sight, sound and touch. So what have we been doing to capture the buyers that are more motivated by sound, why have we been only showing them merely still pictures all this time?

A movie producer will create a movie with an end goal of having as many people watch it as possible, the more that see it, the more money is made. In order to lure the crowds to come watch, the movie makers will create a "trailer" or clips of that movie that make it look as interesting as possible to create great buzz. That is basically what I am talking about and techniques I am using in luxury real estate to take the marketing and promotions of these unique homes to the next level.

Getting back to the story, I will share more about the two vacant mansions in the same neighborhood in the south part of Charlotte. The plan is to make the properties look as good as possible with a top stager, bring them to life with our video crew and team members by showing the homes in use. A good way of doing this is to create a scene entertaining at a party, hosting a business event or charity.

The final crucial step is to use all methods of media as a vehicle to get this video package to as many potential buyers as possible. There are many companies and websites that specialize in the very business of using demographic and geographic searches to create specific pools of buyers that might fit a certain predetermined criteria for you.

About 8 months ago, I was approached by NBC marketing division here in Charlotte and offered an exclusive contract for them to do that very thing for me. They were prepared to create a national campaign by compiling statistics from their exclusive data to deliver my video message to groups of potential buyers. This is exactly what I wanted, to have a top recognized firm delivering my message for me. Regretfully, this did not come to fruition because of my groups budgetary constraints at the time did not lend itself to a company of such large profile. I do look forward to re visiting that topic with them very soon, and creating a very exciting marketing plan.

Keys to Luxury Video Marketing

• Be realistic up front and right off the bat with your listing and marketing expectations. If you know the property is unique and will be hard to sell, don't plan an 18 month marketing strategy. Create a video and media strategy and plan on selling in 6.

• Make the seller aware that a more creative and pro-active method of marketing may be needed in their case, discuss the possible options with them.

• If it will be a big, costly project to film, negotiate them kicking in some of the expense upfront and maybe reimburse them at closing.

• Have a professional crew pre-scouted for the job. Start small, a good camera guy who knows how to edit, and work your way up.

• Be acquainted with secondary video professionals in case you need them. Lighting and sound, aerial video, special audio etc.

• Have a basic understanding of the process and equipment needed for specific job, do your research. Cameras, wide enough lenses, stabilization mounts, dollies, small cranes, tripod etc.

• Sound and lighting must never be an afterthought in this caliber of video. Be sure your crew has proper microphones and lighting for the job.

• Create the video specifically for the house being listed, almost like a short movie. Who will be the audience and what about the house and area do you want them to see? If the house seems dark and isolated, create a light scene of fun and laughter.

• The video can only be as good as its editor!

• Have methods in place, (ie social media expert, websites, marketing company) to help you get your finished video in front of the right audience. This part must be successful.

None of this in any way is re-inventing the wheel, these processes and technologies have been around for quite some time. I am just taking and applying video production methods to the marketing of luxury real estate, the two really go well together in most cases. Many listings will not require me to go to all lengths with the production. A nice $1.1M in Skyecroft, south of Charlotte may only need a brief video in leiu of the standard virtual tour and have it saturate the local area for a quick sell. But a 12,000 sqare foot, $3.2M, all stone Medieval style castle in Southpark may need some special help to keep from sitting on the market for years at a time.

I truly enjoy this very specific niche in the Luxury Real Estate market and am glad that I can share it with property owners who need it, and fellow agents who find it useful and interesting. I very much look forward to the future of video based marketing and feel it will be the way things are done in the world of Luxury Real Estate.

ABOUT THE AUTHOR: *Nick Sylvester*

My career in real estate started about 17 years ago in a bit of a gradual way and has picked up steam ever since. I moved to Southern California after college and graduate school in the mid 90s, and a few years later it all started. The "decade of decadence" I called it, from about 1997-2007 was a time in SO-CAL when everything real estate was like free money and I took great interest in this. At the time, my "day job" was in finance, banking and management positions in "Corporate America" ....you know, the glass highrise with the corner office and the guy with a fancy suit. The pay was good but the hours were long and I just did not find that world rewarding and needed much more in my life.

I think like a lot of people that moved from the snowy Northeast to "Hollywood", I was interested in the film and TV industry from the get go. Spent some time on some movie sets, spent a few weekends as an extra for a few films, met some stars and saw some sights. I met a few friends with some video cam and editing experience and learned a bit but after spending a few Saturdays in "The Troubadour" and "Whiskey a go go", I was not really sure what direction that I was headed.

Time began to pass and I became more involved with Real Estate, mortgage, new constructions, loan origination and everything else that went into the industry. I studied, learned, and worked every area that I could find that included standard sales, foreclosures, short sales, bank-owned property and especially luxury transactions. These were the years that the art of negotiations was mastered with long days caught between the banks, attorneys and clients and their properties. These years were also spent buying, selling and investing in properties on a personal level as well as helping many others do the same. I was involved to a certain extent in the flipping of houses but that was never my passion. During the late 2000's near the end of my California residence, I found myself at "ground zero" of the Sub-Prime Mortgage Lending debacle that all started in Southern California. With heavy pressure from the lending institutions to sell loans so they could turn around and ship them off to oversea investors, we created the "no doc mortgage loans" ...and that was the beginning of the end. I finally left the state in 2007 and headed north for Coeur d'alene Idaho where I planned on buying and investing in lake properties in an area we thought may not be affected by the recession. I spent several years there trying my best in a very unstable real estate market, until the harsh winters and feet of snow proved to be too much for me.

I moved to Charlotte North Carolina in May of 2012, after much deliberation the decision to leave the familiar and head East to raise a family and recreate our Luxury Real Estate business seemed like fate. Charlotte has not been known as a luxury real estate market much in the past but with its constant expansion rate of about 5000-6000 people per month, growing infrastructure, emerging transportation hub, Charlotte is like a blooming flower in the Southeast ready to take its spot as a major metropolitan city. With this expansion, the luxury market here is quickly growing and needs specialized real estate professionals that can cater to the needs of the affluent clientele.

Chapter 13

Viva Las Vegas!

By Albie Vas

Las Vegas, Nevada

I have enjoyed helping luxury buyers, sellers and investors achieve their real estate goals in Las Vegas since 2005. I pride myself in providing excellent customer service and every sale is important to me and my team. I thoroughly enjoy showing people around the Las Vegas area and introducing them to the places that make Las Vegas such a great place to live and invest!

My clients range from athletes, celebrities, local UFC fighters, investors to your native Las Vegans realizing their American dream. Per our fiduciary duties, we never disclose who we are representing unless they make us disclose it first. As with most high-net worth individual, privacy is of the upmost importance and we maintain their strict confidentiality and they are very appreciative.

We have many clients that have relocated from all over the world and it has been our pleasure to assist them. Our priority is to make their move to Las Vegas enjoyable and a smooth transition. In 2013, I procured our toughest listing, a 5,200 square foot, single-story luxury property situated on one acre, located in the suburbs of Las Vegas. As with most transactions, if priced properly, days on the market is not an issue as it will sell quickly. Although this property was priced appropriately, the main problem was the location. The property was located on the very outskirts of Las Vegas. The front of the house faced south and the nearest neighbor to the south was located approximately 250 miles south in Mexico! With the desert surrounding the property, vast wildlife roaming in the area is to be expected. On any given day, you could see big horn sheep running down the street and hear coyotes howling, and even spot a mountain lion. This type of surrounding was unfamiliar to some of our luxury clients. They would fly to Las Vegas, excited to see the property but once they noticed the surrounding area, turn around right away and fly back on their jets.

My team and I worked extremely hard to get this sold! We contacted every one of our clients to inquire if they had any interest or if they knew of anyone that may be interested in purchasing this property. We also offered luxury agents across the nation a 50 percent referral if they could bring a buyer for this particular property.

After six months on the market with no prospects, I realized the buyer would have to be from the Las Vegas area and wanting to be a part of the luxury market. We enlisted the help of our local title company and had them create a list of owners within 3 miles radius of the property. We decided to have an open house and invite everyone from the surrounding areas. We had a great turn out to our open house and even had some invitees arrive on horse-back. I met a very nice couple with 2 small children looking to upgrade to a luxury property. As luck would have it, they lived a half mile from the property. They were very interested in this property! I had them contact my preferred lender to find out if they qualified for a loan to purchase this property. After speaking with the lender, the only way they would qualify to purchase this luxury property was to sell their current house.

The owner of the listed luxury property would not accept a contract that was contingent on the sale of another property. After a long negotiation, the sellers agreed to accept a contingent offer. The buyers enlisted our help and we listed their 3,200 square feet house. With aggressive marketing, we obtained a buyer within 3 days and $10,000 over list price! One of the stipulations of selling their house is that they would close in 2 weeks but would pay rent until they were able to close on the luxury listing.

Now that I had a buyer for the luxury property, it was time for the appraisal. Unfortunately, the appraisal came in $25,000 less than the offered price. The sellers would not budge from the offered price and the buyer was unable to acquire any more funding. I was not going to let this deal fall apart! I came to the realization that it wasn't my commission yet and as we say it in Las Vegas, I was playing with "house money". I represented both the buyers and sellers, and was also selling the buyers' property. To make this deal work, I decide to donate $25,000 of my commission! All parties agreed to the terms and the property closed within two weeks!

Just last week, the current owners of the property contacted me to inquire as to how much the property is currently worth. Curiously, I asked why are they looking to move after nine months – she said we would like to purchase a higher luxury property... and she really hated it when it was pitch dark with a new moon.

ABOUT THE AUTHOR: *ALBIE VAS*

Albie Vas runs the Vas Group, a full service real estate brokerage that has been helping buyers, sellers and investors achieve their real estate goals in Las Vegas since 2005. We pride ourselves in providing excellent customer service and every sale is important to us. We enjoy showing people around the Las Vegas area and introducing them to the places that make Las Vegas such a great place to live! Albie Vas is particularly gifted in marketing, taking full advantage of the power of social media in promoting homes for his clients. The Vas Group has have many clients that have relocated from all over the world. Their highest priority is to make your move to Las Vegas an enjoyable and smooth transition.

www.thevasgroup.com

Chapter 14

Andy's Top 10 Powerful Tools
for Listing Your Luxury Home

By Andy Read

San Francisco Bay Area, California

I sell real estate in San Francisco's East Bay. The properties I sell range from view estates in the hills to warehouse lofts in industrial neighborhoods. The clients I work with are equally interesting and varied. Whether working with local organic chefs, mannequin fabricators, or professional athletes, I have found the following to be crucial when working with listing properties for sale:

1. In a Seller's market, never accept an off-market offer.

Unless you have circumstances that prevent you from wanting your property listed on the MLS (e.g. you are in the middle of a divorce, the property is a mess and you don't have funds to make it presentable, etc.), do not accept an offer "off-market". If the property shows well and is properly marketed, it will almost always sell for more when it is brought to market on the local MLS. Typically, the only person who benefits from this is the listing agent who saves time and money.

2. Ensure your agent uses a professional photographer

Recently, the California Association of Realtors® conducted a study that showed 84 percent of buyers first viewed a property online before going to see it (this number likely now exceeds 90 percent). As such, photography is the first point of contact with your property and will determine whether they visit.

Be sure your broker uses a professional photographer (typically this is an expense paid by the listing broker). Recently there were 47 high-end houses available in Oakland, California on the MLS that had been on the market for 10+ days in a red-hot market climate. 34 of these 47 properties (72 percent) were being marketed with limited or non-professional photography. This is not a coincidence.

3. Be sure to stage or get insight of an interior designer

If your property is vacant, stage! Photographs of empty rooms are not engaging. Even the most imaginative buyers benefit from seeing how a space can be used – the furniture also puts scale to the rooms. We have seen studies (and can confirm from experience) that staging typically provides a return of two to three times the investment. I work with developers who sell new loft/condominium developments. Without fail, the model unit is always one of the first to go into contract. There are countless other examples of properties that generated no interest until they were staged.

4. Make the necessary improvements

If you are looking to get market value or above market value for a property, you need to make repairs to get it as "turnkey" as possible. Depending on the price point, location and style, the repairs and finishes a broker recommends will vary drastically. It is vital to understand the type of finishes to use – do you need Thermador appliances, or will GE suffice? Is it worth the money to use Restoration Hardware for your cabinet pulls? Can you use hollow core interior doors? A good agent will know the answers to all of these.

5. Do not require buyers to remove shoes or wear booties

Often times, sellers want to protect the new flooring they have installed by requiring visitors to remove or put booties over their shoes. For most people this is extremely off-putting and creates an uncomfortable first impression. Prospects and agents don't want to take off their high heels, walk in their stockings, expose the holes in their socks or leave sweaty footprints. Consider the cost of steam cleaning floors an expense of the sale. In addition, hardwood floors are very slippery to folks walking around in socks and I have seen on more than one occasion a person slip and fall creating a liability for the seller.

6. The seller should never attend their own open houses

Resist the urge to attend your own open houses. Nothing good can come from it. Even if you find the opportunity to show a prospect some of the features or give them a personal tour, it comes across as desperate or aggressive. I have seen more than one deal fall out of escrow because of the intimacy created by the seller getting too involved. A buyer is rarely honest with the seller as they don't want to insult them. I have seen multiple deals fall out of escrow because of the false security a seller had based on their conversations with buyers.

7. Inspect, inspect, inspect

Consider inspections as insurance policies. In the East Bay, it is customary for a seller to conduct a home, termite, roof and sewer lateral inspections (and in some cases pool, chimney and structural inspections). If inspectors find that a property "needs" $50,000 of repairs, this information is provided to buyers before they enter into contract and typically protects you from having to reduce your price or credit that amount. On average, I guesstimate that $1,000 in inspections saves a buyer $20,000 in credits.

8. You can never be underpriced in a Seller's market

Too often, sellers get caught up in trying to determine the most equitable listing price. In my opinion, a property can never be underpriced when an offer date is set for offers. Buyers have the same access to the information that real estate agents have and know when a property is a good value. It is usually in the seller's best interest to get more offers with a lower listing price than fewer offers with a higher listing price. I recently bid on an item on eBay that was listed for $1. It was bid on 20 times and sold for $24. Meanwhile, the identical item was listed for $20 and remained available with no bids. Once emotionally invested, buyers can be less logical.

9. Be wary of appraisal contingencies

Though a property is worth what someone is willing to pay, the lenders do not see it that way. If you live in an area where multiple offers are common, be sure to address the potential shortfall in the appraised value before you enter into contract. Otherwise, the buyer is likely to assume the price will be reduced to the appraised value. We recently received two offers on a property listed for $1,500,000 (we thought it would appraise at $1,500,000). One offer was for $1,600,000 with an appraisal contingency; the other was for $1,575,000 with no appraisal contingency. Against my recommendation, the client accepted the higher offer and the property appraised at $1,525,000. Buyer and seller could not agree on terms and it fell out of escrow. It ended up selling for $1,525,000 when it could have sold for $1,575,000.

10. Target your target audience

What is the most likely demographic/psychographic profile of your buyer? Understand who they are in order to properly prepare the home. Should the extra bedroom be staged as an office or child's room? Is the buyer more likely to read National Geographic or Juxtapoz? Do you need to install 220v in the garage for an electric car? Connecting with your target audience is what will separate your property from all the others out there. I recently listed a house in Oakland where the owner had interviewed two other agents both of whom told the owner they had to paint the red walls in the living room to make it more neutral. Understanding that he buyer was likely to be a young "hipster" couple, I convinced the seller to keep them red to give the house personality and best reach the target audience. The property sold $150,000 over the list price and saved my client from having to paint.

ABOUT THE AUTHOR: *ANDY READ*

Andy Read is the Managing Broker and President of Caldecott Properties. Andy was a founding partner of Caldecott Properties in 2005.

Andy specializes in real property sales in the East Bay including single family homes, condominiums, lofts and development sites. Since 2002, Andy has sold $150MM+ and brokered $450MM+ of real estate in the East Bay.

Andy began his real estate career as a licensed Sales Associate in New York for Fenwick-Keats, a residential brokerage in Manhattan. In 2002, Andy moved back to the Bay Area and was a Senior Sales Associate for Lofts Unlimited / Urban Bay Properties in Oakland and San Francisco.

Andy graduated from U.C. Davis in 1996 with B.A. degrees in Sociology-Economic Organizations and Philosophy.

Andy donates a portion of each of his sales transactions to Berkeley's East Bay Humane Society, the East Bay's only no-kill animal shelter.

Memberships, Affiliations & Honors:

- Oakland Association of Realtors®, 2002 - present

- Berkeley Association of Realtors®, 2007 - 2010

- Contra Costa Association of Realtors®, 2010 - present

- North Bay Association of Realtors®, 2010 - present

- California Association of Realtors®, 2002 - present

- National Association of Realtors®, 2002 - present

- Rental Housing Association of Northern California, 2007 - present

- National & California Apartment Associations, 2007 - 2010

- Urban Land Institute, 2007 - 2009

- Commonwealth Club of California, 2007 - present

- Oakland Builders Alliance, Boardmember, 2008 - 2010

- C.A.R. Legislative Liaison, 2009 – present

- ProAgent Magazine "Agent of the Month", January, 2010

- HUD Registered Broker, 2010 - present

- East Bay Symphony Business in the Arts Networking Circle, 2010 - present

- Moraga Chamber of Commerce, 2010 - present

- Oakland Grown, Independent & Locally Owned Businesses, 2010 - present

Contact Andy at www.Caldecott.com

Chapter 15

The Luxury
Resort Home

By Trinkie Watson

Lake Tahoe, Nevada & California

I t's just a matter of zeros! The luxury market can be defined as the top 10 percent of the listed inventory in a marketplace, whether it be the area in general or different residential communities within a city or rural area. In some communities, anything over $500,000 is considered luxury; others it's over $1 million, and in some – like Aspen – it's over $5 million. However, a good luxury Realtor® treats all listings with equal professionalism and attention. Staging, professional photography and well-executed collateral material are a few of the components that contribute to a successful sale.

Selecting a luxury home – whether it be for primary residency or vacation pleasure – starts with location. Primary residency will connect to a buyer's business location and school enrollment. Second/vacation homes can be anywhere…. within reasonable driving distance to the main residence or within close access to an airport, commercial or executive. With all the beautiful places to vacation, competition is strong in the second home market. Sophisticated buyers do not limit their choices. If they are skiers, it's not unusual for the well-heeled to check out the Colorado and Utah resorts along with Lake Tahoe.

With one short stint in the Rancho Santa Fe market, my personal experience has been at Lake Tahoe, California and Nevada. In 1978, I had my first lakefront sale - $125,000 – a home that has long since been replaced with a lovely new structure. In 1980, I obtained my Nevada Broker's license to handle the sales at a new condominium project – Stillwater Cove in Crystal Bay, on the north shore. Consisting of 47 units, ranging from one bedroom to five, this gated community on 16 acres had a beautiful new steel pier with slips and helipad, lakeside clubhouse with restaurant and pool, tennis courts over the garage and on site, and golf carts for access to the units and lakefront amenities. With interest rates at 20 percent, sales were slow but not dead. Because this was a new development, the developer funded all the collateral material and several social events that garnered great publicity and attention. In the beginning, there was no Realtor® cooperation, but after a slow start and picketing because we didn't have a union contractor, the decision was made to join the local real estate board and Multiple Listing Service, giving a bit of a boost to showings and sales. The project sold out in time and has continued to thrive with a strong Home Owners Association.

Following Stillwater Cove, I joined an office in Incline Village, Nevada that focused on high end properties. Few in the business in the early '80s were contacting lakefront owners, so I took on the north and west shores (California) and was successful in listing several nice properties. Unfortunately, with interest rates so high the market was almost dead and nothing sold. However, our marketing was the best….individual flyers and glued-on photographs, something no one else was doing. We developed pages of support description for those interested and ran ads in the local paper. No internet, email or scans in those days. Fax and the US Postal Service were it!

As technology has evolved, it has impacted the way those of us in real estate do business. No longer are we the 'keeper of information' as buyers have access to what's on the market and what has sold and for what price. Frequently prospects know more about a neighborhood than we do because they have been focused there, maybe as a renter or because they have friends who own and want to be near them. This applies to all price ranges and areas. The luxury buyer typically has friends and business associates with whom they communicate about the best places to eat, vacation, shop and travel, so word-of-mouth can have a strong impact on where-to-buy.

The luxury buyer is usually clear and decisive. However, it can take years for the second home buyer to land. Because they are typically successful business people, their focus on a resort purchase is quick and may not return for weeks, months, years. A ski weekend or summer trip to our beautiful lake can stimulate interest in owning. If nothing resonates at the time, you can't give up as persistence pays. My biggest sale took eight (8) years, and I ended up with representing both the seller and buyer. It also included working with the divorcing sellers' respective attorneys and the deciding judge.

The luxury market in our area used to mean being right on the Lake. That has changed with the advent of big names buying our major ski areas....Squaw Valley (KSL) and Northstar (Vail Resorts). In addition, there are several newer golf resorts in the Martis Valley, next to the great ski town of Truckee, that have captured the buyer who wants new product. There are wonderful lakefront properties on both the California and Nevada shores, but beautiful new lake view homes above our shores have also captured buyers that want luxury living away from the main stream.

Probably the biggest challenge a resort Realtor® has is getting sellers to understand that the second-home buyer is being very mindful about what they are paying. Sales are happening in all price ranges, but there is very little competition for vacation homes unless the offering has a fabulous location and floor plan and is properly priced. A challenge for us is the fact that our audience isn't here most of the time. So, when something great comes on and you happen to have the perfect candidate, it's imperative to get the prospect to the table immediately.

Why should someone have a luxury home in the Lake Tahoe area? There are so many great choices for neighborhoods and locations, including states, that it really depends on the interest the buyer has for all the great activities we have to enjoy. Skiers will want to be close to the slopes, boaters want to be on the lake, nature lovers just want the mountain exposure with miles of hiking and biking trails, and families with children focus on Martis Camp, probably the most successful residential resort project in the country. Offerings include everything from the Ritz Carlton Lake Tahoe residences at Northstar – California to understated (as in old) and up-scale glamorous homes on Donner Lake and Lake Tahoe. Those looking to retire eye Nevada, which has no personal income tax. These are the drivers most have for seeking beautiful getaways in all parts of the world.

For the Realtor® looking to engage in the luxury

market, tenacity and investment are key. This is not for the faint-of-heart or pocket. Marketing luxury properties means investing in what you do....not only for personal recognition but for the properties you represent. Luxury home owners expect to see their offerings in print as well as on the web. Being promptly responsive to all communication and staying in touch with owners is huge. One success can build for the next. You don't take a vacation when you close a transaction; you quickly move to generate the next one. The luxury buyers and sellers expect total professionalism. Sellers are busy with their own professions and expect you to be on top of all responsibilities related to marketing and selling their homes. Buyers want you to keep them informed of any new offerings, even if they aren't poised to respond or make a trip to visit. Working with a luxury buyer can take a long time, so be prepared to keep that prospect engaged.

The really great fun and reward of working with luxury buyers and sellers are the interesting people you meet. No question, the financial reward is also great, but those with the ability to buy and sell great properties are intelligent and creative. We are in a service business – the properties are the by-product. So the relationships we develop to assist our clients and customers in seeking their goals are the crux of our business. In the resort market, buyers and sellers come and go, so once the transaction is complete, you may or may not have any continuing contact other than your normal client/customer communication. Get over it. We are no longer their best friend. But, the satisfaction is helping them accomplish what they wanted, and you always want to be available to handle any on-going issues with the purchase or sale.

Selling real estate – at least in California and Nevada – gets more complicated every year. Paper work increases as new law suits get resolved, but it's part of the territory. Selling luxury real estate is a great business and extremely rewarding, but it takes commitment and sincere interest in your clients and customers. To be successful, you can't consider this a job... it's a career for the long haul. I've been doing this for over 40 years....and have no intention of retiring. That's the great thing about our business....you can hang in until you drop! Knowing that we've served our customers and clients in a successful way is the true gold watch when we're ready to hand the baton to the younger Realtor® trained to step into our shoes.

ABOUT THE AUTHOR: *TRINKIE WATSON*

A graduate of UC Berkeley, Trinkie Watson emphasizes the importance of continuing education and has obtained numerous professional designations through the National Association of Realtors® and other related organizations. Keeping up with today-s fast-changing communication modalities is a wonderful adventure which has increased her efficiency and productivity.

With record sales for the Lake Tahoe Region, Trinkie received the prestigious Chase International President's award in 2006. In 2010, she received Chase International's Agent of the Year award. Shari Chase, CEO and President, states "No one knows the art-of-the-deal like Trinkie. She truly understands and satisfies the needs and desires of her discriminating clientele."

As Trinkie says, "The bonus of this business is meeting great people and assisting them with their real estate and lifestyle goals. To go along with that, we have the privilege of representing spectacular properties – from grand estates to lovely mountain, golf and ranch homes."

Among those she has listed include a six-bedroom lakefront home with buoy, shared pier and boat lift; another lakefront home with 11 bedrooms and 14 bathrooms plus a pier and six buoys.

In addition to having served on both the Incline Village, Nevada; and Tahoe Sierra, California Realtor® boards and MLS committees, Trinkie continues community service through the Lake Tahoe Music Festival Board and the Taohe Forest Health System's Foundation Board; the Cancer Advisory Council; and the Orthopedic Advisory council. But that's not all! Her current at-home commitment is an energized, fun-loving German Shepherd named SunDance.

Contact Trinkie at www.TrinkieWatson.com.

Chapter 16

Raving Fans
of Texas

By Donielle (Don) Davis

San Antonio & Houston, Texas

T he National Aeronautics and Space Administration, International flights, the Texas Oil Boom (Eagle Ford Shale), the San Antonio Spurs and Houston Rockets are among the few things that earn San Antonio and Houston, Texas combined the title of "Luxury Home Capitals of Texas!" Over 100 languages spoken, a youthful professional culture and diversity breed prosperity in Houston.

Attracted by the overarching growth statistics, Exxon is expanding operations to the Woodlands near Houston. Not far from the Woodlands, Sugarland offers luxury living to professional athletes along with a sweet easy commute to downtown Houston! Sounds like a great place of opportunity and luxury living. Well, it is!

Many celebrities, professional athletes and executives are relocating to homes in these markets that not only meet their needs, but also bring along an experience and lifestyle. It's also a great opportunity for local and international investors to find a good return on investment through real estate transactions.

To do this, we have to understand what comes first and what is important to our clients. One of the ways we bring those qualities and characteristics out is by asking a few in-depth questions on the subject of luxury lifestyle.

We interview our clients to discover what their most treasured possession is. Notice this is singular because it forces home buyers to examine that one thing they must have and cannot live without. We also ask our clients what is the quality they most desire in a fine product. Without this quality, in their honest opinion, it would not be considered fine. Now, we are really digging deep! What would their ideal floor plan look like if they were to design it? Will it include a Mother-in-law suite? What about an alcove or foyer formal entry? Will the kitchen include invisible appliances and the bathrooms have heated towel racks? When you walk outdoors would it be through a veranda or frameless glass doors? Is there a need for an infinity pool verses a traditional in-ground pool? These are just to list a few things to think about when designing a home and to keep in mind when looking to purchase a luxury home. If luxury changed its name, what should it be called? Is the idea of luxury tangible or a sensation or experience? This is important to know because luxury sometimes is qualified by the history or meaning/value an item has. For example, a basketball is just that, a basketball. A price tag is associated to it depending on where it is purchased. Many people own one. You add Tim Duncan's signature to it and now it has meaning and value. If it was one of the balls he used to dunk or even win the championship with; now we are talking experience and a story. We also need to know if luxury is designated by the area our clients live in - can it be urban (high rises and views) or rural (lakefront and horses)? What luxury car do they consider most overrated? Like beauty in the eye of the beholder, is a luxury car. Is their ultimate luxury time when they spend it alone or would they prefer to entertain friends and family? The answers to these questions help us discover who our clients are and how they relate to people and their environment.

When Listing Luxury Homes, they come in a variety of styles, locations and sizes ranging from Equestrian Properties in Estancia, hill-country views in the Dominion, legacy estates in Alamo Heights, peaceful and natural caverns in Garden Ridge to a Historical home in the "King William-District" San Antonio TX. In Houston, we have water view and golf-course communities like Riverstone, Royal Lakes, Sugar Lakes, First Colony and Greatwood to name a few. We also have Country-club and water-front homes in Sugarcreek, and Cinco Ranch. To attract the right buyer, we must know and market on the features that stand out on the home that are not found or cannot be said about competing properties. This insight or knowledge offers the prospective buyer a sense of Exclusivity and instant Pride of Ownership that results in a successful sale. Remember the basketball? Luxury Home Selling is more than selling a home, we sell a Lifestyle that creates a story that results in a legacy of memories. We currently have 846 existing luxury estates for sale with an average list price of $1,251,524 or $309 per square foot. The average home size is 4052 square feet. And the top seven percent of estates will sell within the next 30 days, according to our price bands, and our marketing consultation analysis.

What do clients say about the Don Davis Realty Group?

"I have relocated over 10 times in my long professional career, and while doing my due diligence on potential (primary residence) properties in the greater San Antonio Area, Don Davis emerged as both a tremendous marketing force and capable real estate professional. My wife and I are prior homeowners in California (3 times), New Jersey (twice), Arizona, Washington State, London, England and Johannesburg, South Africa.

My wife and I first met Don and his team on a 3-day "look see" trip in November 2007. The thing that most impressed me about Don was his detailed qualification process and advance information on potential properties to meet our needs. To tell you a little about myself, I am a 20+ year sales and business development professional in the telecom industry with several dozen multi $M sales to my credit. I take my client-sales relationship seriously and critically, and Don passed the bar on all points.

While conducting the normal drive by and area visuals of all the properties that Don identified based on our specific requirements, he recognized a pattern and trend that caused him to stop the process. He discovered our real needs as upscale buyer's and understood our commute/business travel complexities. The next thing that most impressed me about Don was his understanding of the seller attitude, the buyer (us) attitude, and his role to find a win-win-win solution. Don accomplished this with his patience, flexibility and focus on getting to a positive conclusion to close the deal."

Sincerely, Wilfred Schmedes-VP of AT&T

"It is my pleasure to recommend; Dionelle (Don) Davis - Group Leader of www.DonDavisRealtyGroup.com as a trusted Luxury Real Estate Advisor for any transaction in the state of Texas. Don Davis has provided me and my family with valuable insight on the Texas real estate economy and has exceeded all of my family's expectations in regards to our lifestyle requirements through accessibility, reliability and integrity!

I have known Don Davis for 25 years in my capacity as a friend, teammate (John Marshall High) and as my personal real estate broker at Keller Williams Luxury Homes International. Don Davis has worked with me on various transactions as a Real Estate Advisor-Realtor® and based on his work, I would rank him as one of the top Realtors®' in the country."

Priest Holmes - President, San Antonio/Austin NFL Players Association

Texas Longhorns, (1992-1996); Baltimore Ravens (1997-2000); Kansas City Chiefs (2001-2007).

ABOUT THE AUTHOR: *DON DAVIS*

Donielle (Don) Davis is the Associate Broker and Group Leader of Don Davis Realty Group at Keller Williams-South West Luxury International in Sugarland, Texas. Don is a State of Texas Licensed Real Estate Broker with over 10 years of real estate transactions experience who has assisted relocation clientele from all over the world to The Greater Houston and San Antonio Communities. Don Davis hold's OICP Real Estate Investment Certification Designation from CNN Money's Greg Rand, and also is a member of the ILHM-Institute of Luxury Home Marketing Group, a group of the top luxury agents in the world.

For his group, the gross sales volume has exceeded $50 Million over his career, and his is team has currently have trained over 15 Texas Licensed Real Estate Agents in which experience has ranged from 6 Months to 35 Years on Building a Client 1st Real Estate Business. Our business comes (Word Of Mouth). We simply take care of existing clientele and the referrals keep coming. Don, Texas born and raised, is married to his beautiful wife, Air Force Veteran, Michele Davis, and they have three children, and they are proud members of Pastor Joel & Victoria Osteen's Lakewood Church.

Chapter 17

Luxury Lives in Virginia

By Janet Amendola

Reston, Virginia

T he rolling hills of Great Falls, Virginia are home to some of the most impressive properties in the world. Set between historic Leesburg Pike and the nation's capital and framed by the breathtaking waterfalls of the Potomac River, it's a remarkable place to visit and live. Even when you live here and see these neighborhoods on a daily basis, it's hard not to be taken by the unique architecture and refined landscapes.

The 20,000 SF Elephant...

On this particular day, I was making my way to a 20,000 SF home off Georgetown Pike. As I turned on to the street, the first thing I noticed was the extensive Secret Service detail guarding the home to the left of the property. This is not unfamiliar in this neighborhood, but it does put a slight tension in the air. As I passed along the tree-lined, private drive, and made our way to the front of the home, I was greeted by a stunning multi-level fountain statue and two massive columns that dared me to enter.

I accepted the dare and opened the two story wrought iron and cherry wood custom doors, and immediately gazed at the chandelier hanging in the main foyer. It was a massive constellation of heavy iron and shimmering crystals that had to span at least seven feet wide at its center. As I looked in every direction, my senses were met with grandeur, elegance, extravagance, and custom details fit for a movie set. An oversized chef's kitchen, a huge family room with soaring ceilings and breathtaking windows created a sense of openness that was almost engulfing.

The stately dining room created the perfect flow for formal gatherings and a more private wing on the main floor offered a formal sitting room with some of the most gorgeous cherry paneling and custom shelving I had ever seen. From the crisp sunroom with endless louvered windows to a guest suite with stunning marble and tile details, each part of the main floor was distinct yet made complete sense as a whole.

I made my way to the basement by way of the grand elevator and wherever I turned, I found a perfect marriage of design and function. The 18-person theater, the complete custom wet bar, and a marvelous curved glass wall would have been plenty. Every door I opened was full of new opportunity for a prospective buyer. A commercial grade gym, spa, and sauna would be enough for a professional athlete. Shades of sparkling blue tile work danced along the walls of the spa and I was impressed by the attention to detail.

The upper level of the home lived up to the expectations that were quickly building in my mind. A master suite fit for royalty, with infinite custom wood work and magnificent light features amazed me. Every bedroom in the home was appointed with an en-suite bathroom, each with its own distinctions; from hand-selected marble to beautiful custom cabinetry.

When I reached the main foyer again, I felt overwhelmed by the 20,000 of square feet in this home. No expense was spared and no detail was left unaddressed. And yet, I could not shake the feeling that this home was missing the "je ne sait quoi" that would speak to prospective buyers. The cold open spaces felt lifeless, empty, and far from home.

This architectural behemoth needed a story. It deserved a story.

The story of "The Gatsby House" was born...

After sitting on the market with another brokerage for over 18 months, with only seven showings in that time, the seller called me and my team to explore his options for getting this estate to sell. In that time, the home had sat empty with only a metal chair sitting in the corner of one of the largest kitchens in Northern Virginia. As a Realtor®, you rely on traditional methods for selling a home and cross your fingers that the right buyer comes along. Or, you can innovate. You can make a listing dynamic and you can use every tool at your disposal to bring the right buyer to the home.

As the saying goes, objects in motion tend to stay in motion. This home needed some energy, some excitement, some LIFE. As an agent in a luxury market, the job is no longer to sell property. Until you have a contract in your hands, your job is most inarguably to sell a lifestyle. As we spoke to the seller, I knew this was not merely a matter of adjusting the price or revamping the marketing campaign. It needed a complete re-branding and a big vision. We were looking for the seller to buy in on our strategy. It was bold, it would be time intensive and it would require every resource at our disposal. And, buy in, he did. This is the story of how we sold this home in 45 days, closed in two weeks, and facilitated an international all cash purchase with a Nigerian buyer.

Setting the stage...

On average, home staging provides a 586 percent return on the investment, according to a 2009 Home Gain Survey of over 2000 Realtors®. Fifteen years in real estate have taught me to wholeheartedly believe in the power of staging a home. So, we hired a high end designer and contracted with one of the area's top furniture galleries to bring in the finest furniture and accessories money could buy. We then hired an art broker to coordinate custom art that would tell the story of each room. After weeks of prep work and final touches, the house was starting to take shape and began to summon the emotions I had been thirsting for in my initial tour. And what came next brought this magnificent structure to life.

Lights, camera, action!

According to Domain.com (a premier international luxury listing site), producing and establishing an online video for a property can increase inquiries by over 400 percent. A lifestyle video for a luxury property can capture the emotions of investment-conscious buyers in the $5M and over price point. As we tried to transform this home into a story, we could not shake the idea of "The Gatsby House". We knew the story belied borders and could resonate with buyers all over the world. The concept of old money and new money made sense in this home that had seemed to offer modern ease with classic design. So, we hired the best in the business, held a casting call, and brought in the best hair and make-up crew, costume designers, and after hours of filming our beautiful characters, it was a wrap! The scenes were spectacular in their seduction, but never took away from the grandeur of the home itself. In the end, the 20,000 square feet had a starring role and had never looked better.

The Launch...

We knew the lifestyle video would draw people in through various websites and would reach prospective investors from around the globe. But the goal, in the end, was to get as many well-qualified people in this home to see it in person and experience the details that a video or print marketing would never fully capture. After a classic Broker's Open House event, we kept the party going with "The Launch." We were thrilled to debut this property and its new lease on life. On the guest list were the top luxury brokers in the DC, Maryland, and Virginia markets, their potential buyers, and high net worth locals. Catered delicacies, valet parking, and lively music helped us host a party fit for this home. The cast members from the Gatsby movie attended the party in character and the film was displayed on of the large main walls of the family room. Now people were talking.

The Nuts and Bolts…

Innovation can make a considerable impact on any sale. Finding success in this market means still turning to traditional methods for creating a total package that will truly reach the greatest number of well-qualified buyers possible. From photography to print marketing, even with a launch as impactful as the "The Gatsby House", the strategy is not complete without pushing the marketing to the furthest reaches of the globe and the World Wide Web.

We believe in investing in photographers that have the best SEO'd (search engine optimized) websites on Google so that we are drawing inquiries from every possible angle. We believe in 2D and 3D floor plans and so do most buyers. Eighty percent of home buyers consider floor plans to be essential before viewing a home. Just imagine how effective a 3D floor plan can be in capturing the attention of a buyer across the world.

We all know the value of a professional "take away." With unmatched print quality and professional design, the press printed books we create for our luxury listings are unmatched and appreciated by the pool of high net worth prospects viewing these homes in person and from afar.

In truth, none of these tactics mean much if we do not get the home into the hands of the potential buyers. While networking with our area's top luxury agents and creating the highest quality products is important, the industry is changing and we would be foolish not to maximize the potential of thinking globally when it comes to the luxury market. Our listings are marketed globally using several international MLS systems. We are able to reach 200 countries, in 17 different language, and 22 currencies.

Debriefing success…

There are a couple of invaluable "must-have's" for today's luxury agents…become a Global Property Specialist (GPS), a Certified Luxury Home Marketing Specialist (CLHMS), and a member of the Institute for Luxury Home Marketing. But being an effective Luxury Realtor® goes far beyond experience on paper or credentials. Properties in the $5M+ arena each require the attention of someone with a vision to create an entire package that not only brings it to life, but showcases the property for as many high net worth shoppers as possible.

When you drive down Georgetown Pike through Great Falls and Mclean, on your way to one of the most powerful cities in the world, you notice a lot of for sale signs. And it's true, luxury listings can take a long time to sell. But they don't have to. If you believe there is a buyer for every property, for every 20,000-square-foot elephant, then as a Realtor® in the luxury market, you have to believe in bringing every possible resource to get a property in front of the perfect buyer. In this case, our big vision and passion for innovation not only proved that Luxury Lives in Virginia, It Sells!

ABOUT THE AUTHOR: *Janet Amendola*

After graduating from Virginia Tech in 1997 with a BS in Political Science, Janet decided to make Virginia home. In short order, she found her true calling in real estate. With an uncanny ability to relate to people with diverse backgrounds and budgets, her list of clients grew quickly and organically. Her understanding of business and her passion for helping people is apparent in every transaction. It's not surprising that this depth of knowledge and remarkable interpersonal skills have positioned her as one of the top agents in the industry.

In 2001, with less than two years in the business, Janet was recognized as a Top Producer by the Northern Virginia Association of Realtors® (NVAR). She is ranked in the Top 1 percent of residential sales in North America by Realty Alliance and is recognized as a Lifetime Member of the NVAR Multi-Million Dollar Sales Club. In addition to holding her residential real estate license in the state of Virginia, Janet's designations include; Global Property Specialist (GPS), Certified Luxury Homes Marketing Specialist (CLHMS), Accredited Buyer Representative (ABR), and Certified New Homes Sales Profession (CSP).

In 2012, Janet joined Keller Williams Realty and helped start the award winning "Dwellus" brand. The Dwellus Group is a team of hardworking Realtors® collaborating to redefine the concept of full service realty. Dwellus' innovative marketing strategies and commitment to excellence has propelled them to one of the top teams in Northern Virginia and DC Metropolitan Area. In 2013, Dwellus ranked in the Top 25 nationally within Keller Williams Realty and #2 in the State of Virginia. Dwellus has been nationally recognized by Gary Keller (founder of Keller Williams Realty) as an industry leader. This recognition launched the opportunity to share the Dwellus Group's marketing strategies with 16,000 + Keller Williams agents.

Janet balances her dynamic career with four remarkable children and their numerous activities. In her spare time, you can find her spending invaluable time with family and friends, enjoying a good book, or exercising. Her dedication to community is evident in her many philanthropic commitments, such as working with the Loudoun Abused Women's Shelter (LAWS), where she runs a Women's Life Skills and Leadership clinic.

Chapter 18

Knowing the Right Luxury Home for You

By Erica Glessing

Silicon Valley, California

I was looking at a container of self-contained detergent squares this morning, reflecting on how much it means to get everything right. I like the small self-contained module of detergent because you get it right every time. The module means you place just the right amount of detergent in every wash. When you are buying a home, especially a luxury home, rarely does the science match up like that. The steps to choosing the absolutely right luxury home begin with a strong vision; a clear intention; and then building the right support team around you to achieve the home purchase. Once you have a vision and clarity, don't be afraid to let the energy take you to the right home.

My observations on home sales over the years taught me that when a buyer "clicks" with a home, the click is nearly palpable. The buyer walks in and there is a second sense available that will show the buyer this is a possible right home for them – then the due diligence comes in, but it all goes much easier when the buyer feels that bigger sense of rightness.

Once a home sale is in that mode – the buyer is in place and the seller is alright with the deal conceptually – negotiations have a spirit to theme of "let's get things done," verses when can I jump off this train I didn't want to be on to begin with.

I look for that energy when I meet with sellers – a willingness to accept the right buyer for the property. I look for that energy with buyers – a willingness to recognize when the right home is right in front of them!

In the luxury markets, the buyer might love the same things the seller did about the home, to begin with. It might be the view at sunset or the peaceful surroundings. It might be the gate and the road driving into the home that helps the buyer feel secluded and safe from the fame he or she might possess. Or it might have the perfect high rise location on the perfect street – and the buyer may not even have known he or she deeply desired it until he or she sees it!

I know a wonderful Russian family that worked for

two years to find the perfect home. The separate family room was vital, so they did not look at anything without the family room. When they finally found it, the home didn't have a separate family room! It was on a spacious lot that allowed for plenty of room to expand and with all of the other home features, it was indeed a perfect fit. It just didn't have the family room the buyers so desired – but they were willing to run with the right location and lot and build the home into the perfect home for their growing family.

Think Big and Ask for More

When you are in doubt, ask the home you are thinking about buying "will you make me money in the next five years," or if money is not your greatest value, ask "will you bring me peace over the lifetime I own you," and just keep asking interesting questions and be open to the energy of the answers.

Guidance can leap across the easy specifications and come in the way of a nudge or a sign or a whisper from a friend. If you go visit the home and Paul McCartney is playing on the piano for fun as you walk in, and you love the Beatles, well, you might want to look at the home more carefully. If you have always felt at peace on a lake, but not too close to shore, just above a lake, then watch what it feels like when you walk into the home in that kind of location.

The Right Answer for You

When buying a luxury home, or parting with a luxury home, remember that the answer for you is the right answer for you. It's not about anyone else. Let's say you are selling a second home in Vail, Colorado. And your friends are sad, they loved it when you visited Vail with them every few years over holidays. But now your kids are grown, your skiing days are over, and Vail doesn't feel quite as sexy as Miami or Cape Coral. Let your own needs, wants, desires and wishes be your guide.

Because you may not truly need to be "all about keeping up with the popular people," you can instead become one of the trailblazers or trendsetters yourself. This way whatever choice you make becomes the next sexy choice that others may follow once they see how you stayed true to your energy and your own future vision.

ABOUT THE AUTHOR: *Erica Glessing*

Erica Glessing is the CEO of Happy Publishing, and began writing professionally in 1984. She has published three books on real estate, a half dozen books on self-help and happiness, several novels, and was a top five percent Realtor® at one time with Keller Williams in Cupertino, CA. Her book "Happiness

Quotations" was endorsed by Jack Canfield and Marci Shimoff, and became an Amazon bestseller. You can find her at www.EricaGlessing. com or connect on Twitter or Facebook at "Erica Glessing."

The END

www.ingramcontent.com/pod-product-compliance
Lightning Source LLC
Chambersburg PA
CBHW070530200326
41519CB00013B/3001